Finding Home

Restoring the Sacred to Life

"In this luminous collection of stories by and about homeless women, Anne Scott conveys the sacred power that bubbles from the wellspring of the feminine soul when plunged into groundlessness. Weaving the women's own writing and the recounting of their dreams with Anne's own wise reflections, *Finding Home* is not only a testament to the courage and grace of the women it celebrates, but a call to us all to embrace radical change and bless all that is."

—MIRABAI STARR, author of *God of Love: A Guide to the Heart of Judaism, Christianity and Islam* and *Caravan of No Despair: A Memoir of Loss and Transformation*

"The stories in *Finding Home: Restoring the Sacred to Life* confirm my experience of sojourning our common home for 90 years. Wherever we find ourselves, the heart is where we belong—no matter how estranged we have become. And when we are there, we belong, because what makes home *home*, is that each belongs to all and all to each. I hope Anne Scott's stories from her circles with homeless women touch our hearts and ripple out until all experience our essential belonging."

—BR. DAVID STEINDL-RAST, founding advisor of www.Gratefulness.org

"*Finding Home* is really about remembering "home," the hearth of the soul in every woman whose inner sacred fire is lit by rising spiritual consciousness. Anne Scott privileges us by sharing stories of real women, blossoming out of despair with the realization they are so powerful and dynamic that each can change the world. Women are vessels of Spirit, the life force that heals, and heals the earth, with love."

—KAHOTAKWAS DIANE LONGBOAT, Turtle Clan, Mohawk Nation

"In *Finding Home*, Anne Scott shares the unique, heartbreaking, and yet fiercely hopeful stories of homeless women of all races and ages. These women, like us, hunger for and seek the truest home, and their stories touch a deep chord. Throughout the book, Anne's subtle observations and weavings awaken our own longing for the sacred place within, leading us to genuine contemplation and prayer. This book deserves to be in the hands of social workers, counselors, pastors, and friends and family members of the homeless alike."

—REGINA SARA RYAN, retreat leader, and author of
The Woman Awake: Feminine Wisdom for Spiritual Life

"I picked up *Finding Home: Restoring the Sacred to Life* in the midst of a very active and challenging time of transition in my life —and could not put it down until I inhaled its essence through to the final word. I so needed the healing balm of stillness and love that is the heartbeat of these stories. There is a wholeness about the way Anne Scott has surrendered to this important work on behalf of the feminine that is woven throughout the fabric of her book; that wholeness communicates directly to the sacred center of my being as a woman. Like the women in the circles, I feel deeply seen and known and valued. I can return to face the complexities of my life with renewed stamina because I have been reminded of the truth of who I am. Anne offers this gift to women who find themselves living on the margins of our communities, welcoming them with such authenticity and allowing herself to be awed by their wisdom. Along the way, we all discover grace."

—KATHE SCHAAF, co-founder of *Gather the
Women and Women of Spirit and Faith*.

Finding Home

Restoring the Sacred to Life

STORIES OF WOMEN IN
HOMELESSNESS & TRANSITION

Anne Scott

NICASIO PRESS

First published in the United States by
Nicasio Press, 2016, in Sebastopol, California
www.nicasiopress.com

All inquiries should be addressed to:
Anne Scott
DreamWeather Foundation
P.O. Box 2002, Sebastopol, CA 95473

www.dreamweather.org

Cover design: Patti Buttitta
Interior design: Patty Holden

Scott, Anne
Finding Home: Restoring the Sacred to Life
Stories of Women in Homelessness & Transition

Printed in the United States of America

ISBN 978-0-9818636-8-9

When people tell stories, it heals them.
When we hear stories, it heals us.

—Lyla June Johnston, Navajo Writer

A seed like we

Needs to be given food, water, soil, shelter

And Love from me.

Alone seeds may grow,

But with Love

They are sure to blossom.

—GINGER, living in a homeless
shelter for two years

CONTENTS

PREFACE

THIS BOOK IS A COLLECTION of stories about some of the hundreds of courageous, newly homeless women who have participated in the meditation circles I have led at shelters over the course of the past five years. These are stories of how, when given a safe space to reconnect with the Sacred within themselves, women of all backgrounds and religions can come together to find healing and transformation in the simplicity of silence, sharing, and witnessing.

As I write, not only is there a growing homelessness problem here—and across the world—which is touching more and more people, but there is also a certain homelessness of the soul—of the inner. And so when we offer a place for women to meet and connect at this inner level, while their outer problems remain, they are able to find peace—home, even if just for that hour. Slowly something comes alive in the women through this process. Not for all, of course, because for some the wounds are so deep, and their issues can be complex. But there is usually a healing that takes place, even if it is just a felt experience of being welcomed, as they are having their sacredness reflected.

One morning upon entering a room where we hold our circles, I stop and witness. The stillness is present. A small group of newly homeless women are sitting in silence. Their eyes are closed. In my mind, I see circles and circles of women around the world, linked by a powerful force, going deeper, breaking the barriers between us. Each woman a different race, a different religion, with the world in her heart. Each woman a force of nature—mountain, stream, tree. Each woman stands in her own life, watching her world, our world, come alive, and with grace, be renewed. The stories gathered in this book carry that force and transmit its wisdom.

I have sat in hundreds of circles with women in shelters. Most have been born in this country, but others are from Mexico, Vietnam, China, Germany, Eritrea, Taiwan, Nicaragua, Guatemala, Brazil, Micronesia, and Haiti. They may have come from loving families or difficult ones, but no matter their origins or circumstances, they are connected in the circles by their temporary homelessness and suffering.

Although these women are dealing with great anxiety, restlessness, and sometimes pain, it is a gift to be together with them in deep sharing. None of us are immune to suffering and tragedy in our lives, but these women have had a large dose of it, and they face it—many of them head-on. I am regularly touched by the strength, the wisdom, and the devotion they reveal.

I have changed the names and some of the details in their stories in order to preserve the privacy of these women, but really these stories are relevant to us all. For we are all—women and men, homeless and housed—interdependent. We are all, each in our own way, longing for home. And we are all engaged in this work of weaving back into consciousness a deeper way of relating to life and its sacred source.

INTRODUCTION

As I HAVE SAT WITH WOMEN in circles over many years, I have continually seen that I am not alone. Some of these women have lost everything and are newly homeless. Others have homes and possessions. Whether our life circumstances are similar or appear to be significantly different, there is a common thread that connects us all— our longing for the sacred within. This yearning is like a song nearly forgotten, but not quite.

I remember the woman from Brazil, a former Montessori teacher who had moved to California to be with her son. The first time she sat with us at a shelter, she listened intently while I explained the purpose of the circle, and then said, "My grandmother had wisdom. My mother had wisdom. I do not. And I am lost."

There is a need at this time, according to elders from many traditions, for women to help bring the sacred feminine back into consciousness, where it can heal and nourish life. The knowledge that we seek is inside us and in our relationship to life. Our honoring of silence, sharing, and witnessing brings forth wisdom and transformation. In listening to each other's stories, we find extraordinary beauty. This beauty opens to the sacred feminine, which is vital for the evolution of consciousness for men and women alike.

In a circle, there is no leader. We each have different life experiences and different circumstances. We sit as equals— a clan of teachers witnessing the inner world together. How does the circle work? Imagine a pitcher of water. If there were no container, the water would spill everywhere. A circle contains. It embodies the feminine—the power of holding and receptivity that restores the whole.

I spoke at the 2015 World Parliament of Religions on a panel with seven other women from diverse cultures and spiritual traditions. I had five minutes to talk about embodied service—what it means for a woman. I hadn't prepared a talk (none of the women had)—words just came from the heart.

Many years ago, I said, when I first began to hold circles for women, I stood outside under a full moon, and asked silently, in prayer, what was to be the focus of my work. I felt no response, and went to sleep. That night I had a dream.

In the dream I saw the Earth, a beautiful, blue Earth in the darkness of space. Then I saw red, inflamed areas on the surface where there was violence or war. I suddenly noticed a full moon on my right. Soft rays of light streamed down, touching like a balm on the inflicted areas on the Earth. And I heard these words: *Wherever the feminine touches, there is healing.*

The healing power of the feminine was to become the focus of my work over the next twenty-five years, both in this country and internationally. But over the years, I began to wonder: is it only in comfortable circles that we can experience this healing light? What about those places at the margins of society, where women are floundering on the edge?

I approached a women's day shelter and was invited in. There I met marginalized women whose spirits pined for something so close, yet so far away, a yearning almost erased by our contemporary life. Many doors had closed for these women, but sitting together in circles, they found a way to understand their soul's longing. They used their imagination to ease their despair. They took steps to create lives out of their own feminine nature. They crossed from one stage to another—from isolation to connection, from loss to a sense of meaning.

Gradually, I found that I had to "do" less and less in these circles. But sometimes I would have moments of doubt about their effectiveness. On those days, I would silently ask that I be a conduit, so that the women could be given what they needed. And then I would get out of the way. No ideas, no agendas. Just sit with them, listen to their stories, share in the silence, and guide them in writing exercises. Over time, several colleagues volunteered to join me in this work.

In these pages, I share my experiences over many years of witnessing women connect to their deepest being. They do this by creating space for themselves and one another. They meditate, listen, and, in the stillness, find inner knowing and healing.

Before I continue, I would like to share an experience. One day, a few years before I began to work with newly homeless women, I was camping in the Sierras. Early one morning, my husband had gone for a swim in a nearby hot spring. I decided to walk into the pine forest.

I noticed that many of the trees were not thriving; the branches were brown. And then I realized that this was sacred land. I suddenly felt the suffering of the Earth. I knelt down and cried. I had never experienced such a wave of sorrow. It did not feel personal. I asked the Earth for forgiveness. Forgiveness for ignorance and greed, and how we have damaged the Earth. And when the tears stopped, I began to sing to the land—lullabies that I once sang to my own children many years ago when they needed soothing.

When I stopped singing, I felt quietness deep inside— a peace. I turned and walked back to our tent. I lay down and fell into a deep state of sleep. And then I had a vision of a Native American man striding toward me out of the darkness. He handed me a walking stick with a feather tied onto it, and then receded back into the darkness.

I told no one of this vision until several years later when I hosted a conference and invited a Blackfoot environmental scientist to speak. After the conference, I drove her back to a small town where she stayed with a friend. We took a walk on a suburban street that was just minutes from the rolling hills that surround the Pacific Ocean. I felt a deep kinship with her, as we spoke about her presentation and the courage it had required. For she had shared with over a hundred women a dream she had had during her time of scientific research. How two worlds had collided inside of her, giving her access to profound insight and compassion.

With just a few minutes left before I needed to return home, I told her my vision. She stood in silence for a minute or so, the native grasses waving behind her from a garden. And then said, "You honored them. So they honored you. Women are the Earth. That's why the healing work with women is so important." I then understood that my vision had been a type of blessing to do this work with women of all backgrounds and traditions.

Just as the Earth needs healing, I feel strongly the need for women to heal and bring forth the light that is hidden within them. The qualities that the women's circle awakens are not valued in our culture for the tremendous power they bear: Listening, Beauty, Stillness, Attention, Holding Space, Longing, Healing, and Belonging. Each are facets of the Sacred. And we need them.

STORIES

⫸⫷

LISTENING

The last time at meditation I felt so peaceful. I talked about the pain in my heart. You listened. This lifted something. I feel no burden, no weight. I feel so light, my heart is healing here.

— ALANA, newly homeless, living in a shelter for one month

I come here for the quiet. There's so much noise in the shelter, and here I can be quiet, and listen inside.

— TERESE

THE RIVER OF LIFE

JACKIE WAS WEARING JEANS and a sweatshirt the first time I saw her. She bounced into the room full of life, looking much like any young woman in her twenties, and took a seat in the circle. I found out later that she is in her late thirties, a mother of two teenagers. A month before we met, she had fled her home and moved to a shelter in the vicinity to protect herself and her children from neighboring gangs. She had felt a prisoner in her home and could never go to the store or do her laundry without harassment. Jackie came to the day shelter where I hold circles.

We know nothing about a woman at the moment she sits down with us in the circle. Little by little, she begins to open. On that first day, Jackie said she had never meditated, and thought she'd try it. This is a short, silent meditation of the heart. There is a feeling of restlessness when a woman first meditates. She may find it difficult to sit still. Feelings that have been rejected sometimes surface. But when I say that we will meditate for just five minutes, the women seem to relax more easily. After a minute or so, there is a feeling of stillness.

My own eyes are closed, but I sense the atmosphere in the room. It has a texture that one can recognize and identify. Not with words, but with a feeling for the energy among the women in the room. I ask the women to think of someone they love, or a special tree or a beloved pet, and to put this feeling of love into their hearts. The women do this in their own ways, but invariably they come to similar places of stillness and peace. I suggest that if troubling thoughts come up, or busy thoughts, or difficult feelings, that they drop the thoughts into their heart like pebbles into a lake.

Jackie, like the other women, went into silence. This was her experience:

> *I saw rose petals swirling down in a spiral and going out over the ocean. I found a really calm place. I saw a man who was very strong, and I was a little afraid because he wanted to give me a massage. But he touched my feet. And I wasn't afraid anymore. I didn't know this was inside me. I saw these images—they help me. I feel calmer. This was cool!*

Afterwards we spoke about the need for her to reconnect to a nourishing masculine. This inner masculine strength in a woman is the energy that carries her into the world. Without it, a woman cannot manifest what lives in her soul.

THE SPIRAL

Jackie returned a month later. On this day, I showed the women an image of a nautilus shell. I talked about how a spiral moves into the center and then out again, about how there is both darkness and light in the image. I handed out paper and pens and asked the women to write freely, beginning with the words *Once there was a spiral*. This was the first time that Jackie experienced the writing practice. She wanted to try it.

> *Once there was a spiral storm, a spiraling storm, my old home. They say there is the calm before the storm, but for me now, it is after the storm that my calm began to come.*

After writing this, Jackie shared about her life before going to the shelter. Early one morning she had packed her family's belongings in two duffel bags, leaving behind furniture, books, flowers and house plants that she cherished. She had left everything behind because she wanted freedom for herself and for her children. She told us about her goal of studying culinary arts so that she could teach others how to cook healthy, ethnic foods. She already knew the properties of ginger for digestion, chamomile for calming the mind, and other herbs that have medicinal qualities. This had been her passion for a long time.

After reading aloud about the spiral, she said that now she felt free "to reach the potential that God has for me."

THE OCEAN

Two months later, Jackie came to our Thursday meeting. This time Jackie was wearing black trousers and a fitted jacket. Her work clothes, she said. She had asked her boss for this day off. She needed to experience the calmness in our circle. Unlike in the past, when she would have talked in a joking way, this time she went into meditation without saying much beforehand.

The ocean image returned to her as a place of peace, and inner strength. As she shared after the meditation, she didn't put spiritual terms to it, but spoke as if a sacred presence will always be there for her.

I have found that when a woman is held in the safe container of the circle, when her essential nature is recognized and acknowledged, she becomes conscious of her inner knowing. Even traumas can be held and often healed in this sweet place inside a woman. And if needed, she is free to share about the trauma in the circle. But this rarely happens. Sometimes a woman touches the edge of a trauma, with a hint or in a story. It seems that no more is needed. In the silence that follows, sometimes a woman weeps. Always, we listen.

Over the next seven months, Jackie came sporadically to our circle. With a new job, and starting classes at the junior college, she was busy. But when she felt a need, she came to our meetings. Her smile lit up my heart every time she entered the room. The women's meditations and conversations opened up a new avenue for her and grace unlocked new potential.

When she sat with us, she showed an eager curiosity about her life. She was in love with her children, so proud of them, and proud that they had accepted leaving a violent neighborhood for the security and safety of a shelter. She spoke tenderly about how they knew they needed to do their best. One of them starred on the basketball team, and the other volunteered at an after-school program for younger children. The last time I saw Jackie at the circle, she said that in meditation she found a feeling of peace. "Now," she said, "I know my next step."

Reflection

What is it in Jackie that made her act to save herself and her children? Is it grace or timing? Or is it listening to something inside that gave her the power to make a step?

Perhaps her realization came from innate wisdom, perhaps from a spark of the divine feminine. Having an interim safe place to go to, and being with women helping other women to find their strength and value—these helped her connect to the riverbeds of life, which enable a flow and depth in our lives.

Jackie knew the time would come for her to find another place for her family because, after six months at this shelter, all women must move on. When she went to see about transitional housing, the organization that provides it was so impressed by her that they shortened the normal waiting period of six months to two. Jackie now has a home for herself and her children.

STILLNESS

The quiet and stillness helped me to focus on where I'm going. To be straight and direct and not go sideways and be distracted.

—ESTHER, living in a shelter for three months

꙲꙲꙲

For the first time I was actually able to let my mind empty. Usually my mind goes into hyper drive. This meditation was different. Peace, tranquility, patience, were in abundance.

—PATRICIA, living in a shelter for one year

꙲꙲꙲

I didn't understand what you meant by stillness. But then I realized that I had some kind of knowing. When I see the beauty of my children sleeping next to me, that is my stillness.

—NATIVE AMERICAN MOTHER of a three-year-old and a five-month-old child

DROPPING RESISTANCE

ELEVEN BLACK WOMEN and one white woman living in a Baton Rouge homeless shelter walked in quietly to our gathering space. Most of them wore trim slacks and a fashionable blouse with jacket or sweater. They made no eye contact with each other or with me. Like women I have met elsewhere in shelters, they were not recognizable as newly homeless, but I was particularly struck by their being. Distant, and somehow, inaccessible.

They congregated around the coffee and muffins, beginning to talk to each other, but still avoiding eye contact. The director of the center invited them into the sitting room where the workshop would begin. I felt like an outsider, unsure of how things would develop that day. As the women took their seats, they formed a circle. The youngest—perhaps in her late twenties—was wearing a huge white headset over her ears. She stared at the floor. The others folded arms in front of chests or crossed legs at the knee.

I wondered if I had been naïve to think that our circles in Northern California were transferable to a different region of the country. The executive director made an introduction, welcoming the women and me. I took a deep breath. I had no choice but to be real with these women. The room was quiet; they waited for me to speak. What came was a story.

A few years ago I attended a global peace confer-ence in Geneva, Switzerland. I heard stories from around the world—details of the impact of con-flict or war on women's lives in Palestine, Israel, South Africa, and other countries. For four days, I listened to these stories. Of a pregnant woman unable to pass through a check-point to get to a hospital in order to give birth. Of a lack of basic necessities, such as prenatal vitamins, food, men-strual pads, and education. Of refugee camps and violence. On the last day of the conference, I sat on my bed in the hotel room and cried. But then I realized I had come half way around the world for this conference, so I returned to the main hotel for the closing ceremony.

The ballroom was filled with an audience of three-hundred people—ambassadors, social work-ers, women from non-profit organizations, all conference participants. When I walked into the room, the Tibetan nuns in their orange robes were standing before the applauding audience. They bowed deeply several times and then returned to their seats. The conference convener asked the Af-ghan women to come forward. These courageous women had left their country in the middle of the night to avoid arrest. Again, the audience clapped loudly.

The honoring of women continued as those from Rwanda, South Africa, Maori from New

Zealand, all came to the front. For the first time in four days, joy filled the room. In the midst of the suffering that was taking place around the world, we witnessed those who had found a deeper form of empowerment.

I looked around at this circle of women from Baton Rouge. Their arms had unfolded. Legs uncrossed. Their resistance gone. This story had lifted their shame. I asked the women to share their names, and why they were here at the workshop. As they ventured to speak about their lives, slowly the tension dissipated, and I could feel my own heart soften and open to them.

FOUNTAIN OF LIGHT

After a lunch break, we moved to a larger space for the remaining hour-and-a-half of the workshop. The room was empty of all except a circle of chairs, and in the center, greenery and a large candle burning. Brickwork lined the walls, the floor, polished oak—creating a quiet feeling, like being in a grove.

I spoke briefly about my own life. How difficulties had opened me to a realization of the wisdom that lies in every woman. How this wisdom comes through dreams, or contact with an inner knowing that begins to inform our lives and guide us.

I described a simple meditation of the heart, and then

we sat in silence for seven minutes. I had no idea what was taking place in the women, but there was a deep feeling of calm in the room. As soon as I ended the meditation, a woman who had earlier said she was once a schoolteacher raised her hand to speak.

I heard two words, "Award. And Peace!" What was this? How could this come out of me? I've been praying for the last few months, to have peace. But what was this?

Bursting up like a fountain of energy, the women then began speaking. They might not have called it their sacred nature, but they were affirming to each other, sharing in a heartfelt way, the wholeness that still exists within, no matter what they have experienced in life. The vitality in the room shone through them.

When the workshop was over, the women, animated with a sense of warmth, gathered their belongings. As I stood up, the woman who had been the most antagonistic of them all approached. Something had changed. Her face was open, soft.

She said, "I saw light in the meditation. What *is* that? I've never seen anything like that before."

"That's *you*," I said.

Her face registered surprise, and she nodded, thoughtfully. Slowly, without a word, she turned and walked away. Just then the young woman who had been wearing headphones the entire morning, stood in front of me. Her headset was in her hands. She gazed with her deep, dark eyes, completely unguarded, into my own.

She said nothing, but continued looking at me. After a long minute, I reached out and held her hands. I wondered what she was trying to say in this silent communication. I remained open, and then, instinctively I knew that she was showing me her innocence.

This is a place inside every woman, a place that precedes healing. A place uninjured and inviolable. It is from here that the wounds of violation can be healed. When I finally understood this, I said quietly, *Thank you.*

I could bear witness to her sorrow. I could open to the aliveness of her soul, the beauty of her being.

Reflection

Was this experience for the women from the Baton Rouge shelter to be lasting? Two months later, I called the program director.

> *It was a glorious day. They loved it so much. The day after, the women really got sharing heart to heart stories with each other, trusting the commonality of all of us. Everyone appreciated the experience.*
>
> *We now have two days a week of morning meditation, ten to fifteen minutes to enjoy the silence and quiet. The women love the silence. I tell them, "Close your eyes and relax, breathe deeply,*

just like you showed us. Focus on the inner wom-
an within yourself." Two or three have found jobs.
It was very positive.

So I learned that what happened that day did not just come and go. It remained and lives on in the women who participated, as it lives on in me. This reservoir of wisdom that women tapped into, astonishing us with its power and depth, is in fact not out of the ordinary. It is just that somehow in our culture we have forgotten the presence of grace.

THE VOICE WITHIN

AVA APPEARS ONE DAY at our circle at the shelter in Northern California. "Where've you been?" she asks. "We were looking for you." It has been a year since I last saw Ava in a different shelter where we had offered an eight-week pilot program. Ava was a former Montessori teacher from Brazil. I met her when she was just two weeks homeless. Now, a year later, she looks weary.

I say I've been here at this day shelter every Thursday since I last saw her.

A tree trimmer buzzes a chainsaw outside in the parking lot. I try to explain the meditation, but feel uneasy about the noise that might distract us and make it more difficult for the women to relax. The sound of the chainsaw penetrates the walls of our sitting space, and then there are new sounds of people walking on the roof. We meditate anyway, and the sound of the chainsaw fades.

Afterwards, several women say it was not so difficult to sit still despite the noise. A few of the women begin to tell about their lives and how important it is for them to be able to listen inside.

I notice Ava because she is leaning forward in her chair, listening so intently. I remembered this quality about her from a year ago. I felt her engagement deeply and had always liked having her in the circle. I don't know much else about her life. Towards the end of the meeting, she asks for the talking stone.

A woman who holds the stone knows that she has the space to speak. No one will comment. We just listen. Ava wants to know more about listening, she says, and passes the stone back to me.

I decide to speak about how I used to walk along the rural road near where I lived. It was a time for me to listen inside, and to the wind in the trees and the sounds of hawks. It was a time for me to heal and pray. I took my silent early morning walks for ten years.

When I finish, Ava reaches for the talking stone. She looks at it carefully, her fingers lightly touching the polished, heart-shaped green malachite, and speaks.

As you talk about the silence and listening, I realize that's what I have been trying to find at the shelter. There's so much noise. So I get up at 5:30, when it's still dark, and go to the other end of the parking lot near to some trees. I get very silent and go into the depths in myself. Now, from what you are saying, I realize that there is always a voice whispering to us, trying to help us to make the right decision. I made many wrong decisions.

And often I did not listen because it is very subtle, and when we are afraid, or stressed, we can't hear it. But it's always there, whispering—it has the answers deeper than the ego. We don't listen because we are so emotional, or too busy. Only now I am learning to listen to that voice.

I was afraid to go into that deep place—the divine.

SHE LET GO AND SHE FLEW

IN OUR CIRCLES, we hold an empty space. We do have some tools to help with this, especially when the group needs to focus.

It's simple, I suggest. We will write for a few minutes, and then later, you can share what you wrote if you want. Or, you can keep it for yourself if it's something private. Just let the writing flow without trying to make it sound good.

Ginny, my co-facilitator, usually closes her eyes while the women write. There is always a quality of creative stillness, as if the women stand at a doorway, allowing what is inside to flow out. The inner world, usually so distant, comes close enough for the women to sense its sacredness.

Ginger, who joins the women's circle at the shelter where we hold our weekly groups, says, "I need the quiet. It's the only place where I can listen inside."

When I first met Ginger, she sat slightly curled, hunched over. Over the months, she began to dress in brighter colors, and she stood taller. There was a new sparkle in her face. She brought joy to the circle.

Over the course of a year, she attended regularly, except for one month. When she returned to us, she explained what had happened.

I found a housemate and moved into an apartment. It was okay at first, but then he became loud and abusive. I didn't know what to do and didn't have the strength to do anything. But then one night I remembered the silent meditation I learned here. I sat in my room and grew very quiet. And then I realized what I needed to do, and I was able to leave.

On this day, I initiate the writing exercise and, after six minutes have passed, I wrap it up and ask if anyone wants to read what they wrote.

Ginger says that she will read. But before she does, she tells us that she will be moving into her daughter's house. Their relationship has healed. This is her last meeting with us, she says. During the writing exercise, she wrote out a poem that had come to her this morning, while walking to the shelter from the bus stop.

There was a bird
learning to fly
afraid to fall
a voice from above
you can do it, she heard
she let go and she flew
it just took one word
of encouragement.

PEACE

"I DIDN'T ASK to come here," says Tanya as she saunters into the room. "I'm just here 'cause Celeste told me to come." Celeste, the day shelter's program director, has a refined sense of who might be helped by the circle.

"You can leave if you'd like," I say.

But Tanya says she will stay, at least for a while. I read to the women before we meditate. It is a statement from an Aleut elder, Larry Merculieff. He says, "Silence opens us to our inherent intelligence."

Tanya interrupts. "What *is* this, voodoo?" She laughs.

"It's just a way to calm ourselves and listen inside. You don't have to meditate if you don't want to."

Tanya shrugs. There's a moment of quiet. Then Tanya says that she has never sat still in her life. Never sat in silence. But she wants to know what meditation is like.

As the women close their eyes and settle, they drop into the silence. There is such a complete stillness that I wait for an extra few minutes before ending the meditation. It has been about seven minutes. *Peace be with us*, I say, to end the meditation.

Tanya opens her eyes. She is crying. "What *was* that? I felt peace. I never felt anything like this. I came here to *dis* you white ladies. I didn't know this was possible."

Just last night, she says, she had the thought that she wants to come clean. Tanya had been praying the night before. She'd been praying *for the first time*, she tells us. She loves her children, and is afraid they would be taken away if people knew that she abused alcohol.

"Well," I say, "Looks like your prayer was answered."

We never saw Tanya again at the shelter.

Reflection

Sometimes I see these major shifts in women, like glimmers of light. Yet, I might never see some of them again.

There is no doubt in my mind, that these mini-transformations are powerful for the women. But that day, as at other times, I questioned the practical effectiveness of our program for women like Tanya, who are less motivated, or who have more complex issues than those who come regularly. When I held a question such as this, inevitably, the next circle would show me how I was misguided in thinking so causally. For the work is not linear. Its power lies in the potency of simply holding the circle weekly, sitting with the women, regardless of how often they return. With time, the circle itself grows stronger, seeming to carry its own energy.

One day, two weeks later, Celeste walked over to me after the circle. "You remember Gina? She's in Heavenly Treasures." This clothing store, connected to the shelter, provides jobs for the women.

I did remember Gina and a quality about her that I couldn't pin down, something refined like a keen intelligence or unusual sensitivity. She had come only once to the circle and said little, if nothing, about herself.

In Heavenly Treasures, I found her towards the back of the store, hanging up clothes on the rack. Her face lit up when she saw me. "Thank you for coming. I wanted to be there today but I had to work. I told Celeste that the meeting was the most important thing that happened to me. I read your book three times. It's been so valuable. Thank you."

"I can't speak about it, but I found something precious." Ever so briefly, she placed her hand on her heart.

She explained how the shelter and social workers helped her to relocate. She now had housing. "In the circle, someone told a dream about a baby," she said. "I realized something about my own life from that dream. It changed me."

HEALING

You don't know how important this circle is. It's the first time I've felt safe among women. I know I can say anything and you won't judge me. I can think here. I grew up in an orphanage, and learned not to trust women. I felt so alone. There are so many people and so little connection. But after the meeting, I felt like I was connected.

— TATE, homeless for four months, living in a shelter

TIME TO LOOK INSIDE

RACHEL WALKS INTO the small room where we are holding a new circle at the largest shelter in the county. She appears to be middle-aged, and wears pink hair curlers and a pink sweatshirt. In the first few minutes, as the women introduce themselves, my heart opens to Rachel. When it is her turn to speak, tears come to her eyes.

> *I'm not a complainer, but it's been a huge transition to be in a shelter. I'm sorry for crying. I moved to the shelter a week ago with my son who's twenty-eight. We were living in our house but my husband died a few years ago and then we couldn't pay the mortgage. We've been living in a motel but the money ran out.*

We listen. I have a sense that the other women are having a similar response to mine. Our hearts are stretched wide. I realize that I had judged her in that first moment, wondering why she had come to a meditation meeting. It was the pink hair curlers. But now I feel only compassion.

I turn off the overhead fluorescent light and leave the small table lamp on. It gives off a dim light, enough to see the women but not to see their faces clearly. The candle flickers on a side table.

I invite the women to close their eyes, and to breathe evenly, like the ocean waves, ebbing and flowing gently. I describe a meditation they could try.

Several women sigh, and then the room quiets. After a while, I open my eyes to check the time but can't read my watch. I glance up and am quite startled. There, sitting opposite me in the circle, sits Rachel. Her head leaning back, and her face seeming to be completely relaxed, a slight smile on her lips. I close the meditation, and the women open their eyes. The room is quiet, and warm. I decide not to turn the overhead lights on.

Several women on my left say that the meditation made them feel calmer. Then Rachel speaks, her face alive, as if something astonishing has happened.

I saw blue. A wall of color—blue with a little green. It made me feel so peaceful, so calm. It was just incredible peace. I didn't know this was possible. I've been working all my life. I started work when I was thirteen. I'm fifty-three now. I've never had the time to look inside. I never thought about it.

THE BUSH

A week later, Rachel arrives first to the circle. She wears khaki slacks and a blue sweater. She looks fresh and cared-for, her short hair neatly combed. "I'm excited to be here," she says.

All the women who had been at our previous sitting arrived. I suggest we skip introductions and go straight to meditation. Afterward the women speak briefly. They use words like relaxation, and peacefulness. Then Rachel says that she wants to tell us what she saw during the meditation.

It was like a dream. I was flying high above the earth. And then I came closer to the ground and saw a small bush! It was dried up and barely alive. Does it have any meaning?

I ask Rachel what is her relationship to plants. She thinks for a moment. Her late husband didn't trust her with watering. He used to say she has a black thumb and wouldn't let her near their garden.

"What if this bush is *inside* you? A part of you that needs water and attention," I suggest.

Rachel looks puzzled. No one speaks. The room is quiet until Carmen, a bright young woman who was born in Mexico, leans forward.

"It *means* something. You're gonna grow! One day you'll find out what that bush is. You'll know how to care for that bush!"

"Yes," I say, "there's a place inside us that needs our love and attention. It can help us in our life. It calls to us, sometimes through a dream, or an image, just like Rachel's bush. Inside each of us, there's the knowledge of how to care for this place within."

It is ten-thirty on a cold, foggy February morning, and it's time to close the circle. The women are lively as they leave. Rachel has a brightness in her face, like someone who has just discovered new hope.

Reflection

After the circle, my awareness was on the wonder of what had just happened. As I gathered up my books, put the candle in my bag, and walked down the concrete stairs to the ground floor, I noticed the same artificial iris in a pot on the window sill that I had seen in the morning, but it no longer felt bleak. And outside, the abandoned railroad tracks lined with weeds, did not seem empty. I realized that the circle is growing stronger.

COMING BACK TO WISDOM

ONE DAY, I talked with Nancy, another co-facilitator, over tea. How did she experience the eight-week program? I asked. After a moment's pause, she answered.

> *I see that women often feel wrong. How they are doesn't fit anywhere. So we sit with the women so that they can uncover and come back to their wisdom. A little space is all that's needed.*

The conversation deepened, and Nancy, a nurse who has worked with women for over thirty years, spoke of hidden feelings that took time for her to understand.

> *Being with the women living in a homeless shelter terrified me. It touched a place deep inside of me that has carried the fear that ultimately I will not be provided for—that I will be homeless. It was too frightening to think about, and there I was sitting with women living homelessness. I know somewhere inside myself that by facing the women I was facing a primitive fear in myself.*
>
> *I call this fear primitive because for me it is a fear carried by the feminine. It is not derived from my life. I understand that homelessness for the feminine is a characteristic of an early stage of*

development. The feminine was at home in itself, but because it was not valued, it has found itself homeless.

The women living at the shelter are carrying this wound and living it openly in the world. I recognize what they carry for all women.

LOVE UNDER THE BRIDGE

ONE DAY at our meetings for newly homeless women, one of the women admits that her worst fear was that she would end up living under a bridge. There are seven women that day in our circle. On the wall opposite where I sit is a painted rainbow in muted colors. There are baskets of shells, crayons, and Sunday school books on the low shelves at the end of the room. Outside the window, children play on swings and a seesaw in the garden. The woman shares that on the day her daughter asked her to leave, she was gripped with fear of homelessness. She tells us what she had thought to herself as she left her daughter's home. "Oh God, please don't make me live under a bridge."

Next to her sits Isabel who was born in Guatemala. She lives with her husband in a house, and volunteers at the shelter because she has been homeless herself. Until now, Isabel never talked about herself in the circle. She speaks quietly.

> *I lived under the bridge. I lived there for months. If I can survive that, I can survive anything. Because of my time there I became whole. I am now whole. I met my husband there. He said to me, why do you live in the past? Why can't you forgive your first husband? So I forgave him one night and then my life began to change. I can live in the present now.*

My first husband died, he was from Mexico. My second husband died here. I had a nervous breakdown. I was taking drugs for depression. The doctor gave them to me. Then I couldn't afford them anymore and now I am well.

That is my experience. I believe I am here for a purpose. Nothing happens that doesn't have a purpose. Now I volunteer and tell people things like what a nice dress someone has. We have to be kind to each other. To help each other. I have wisdom now. I am 53. I did not have wisdom before. But now there is something else. I see how life works differently.

Reflection

After four years of coming to our circles when she had the time, Isabel tells the women one day that she wants to become sober. Our circle is not a recovery group but is an empty space where the women are held, seen, and loved. We hold the hearts of the women, in the midst of all difficulties, all sorrows, and all transformations.

This announcement of Isabel's makes me reconsider who comes to the circle. In the beginning of our circles, I had explained to the program director that the meetings were to help women who were ready to make a step. I had carefully drawn boundaries to keep out women with severe mental illness, and women who had addictions. This work is not for them, I told her.

But in fact, women came who needed it, regardless of whether they had mental illness or were struggling with addiction. They came and, simply through being in the space, experienced an innate respect for what was present and, through time, a type of healing they were in need of. In all five years, we have needed to ask only one woman to leave the circle.

Over the years I have come to understand how women are drawn to the sustenance they need—to the inner or spiritual food that is essential, like the roots of a tree reaching downwards to groundwater below. Women like Isabel have needed a place such as the circle. These women are sacred beings, even if no one has ever reflected to them their sacred essence. When this is honored, something comes alive.

So it has been for Isabel. "Little by little, as I listened to you and the women, I learned to love myself. Even though I have learned many things in my life, I didn't know that I needed to care for myself. This I realized when I became quiet."

Another woman, Teresa, comes to mind. Teresa has been faithfully attending our circles on and off for two years. Most of the time, when she comes, she cries. A severe childhood with a psychologically disturbed mother had created a complex condition. While it seems we do nothing in our circle, in this nothingness, something is happening.

For a woman such as Teresa, the terror of the wound begins to be contained. No longer does she speak at length about her past. She comes, she says, to experience inner peace. And this is what she finds, every time, even if for five minutes, or half an hour. This peace is her touchstone. We do not know if she will ever be fully functioning. But for most women, there is a stabilizing effect of the circle.

COMING HOME

ON A COOL September morning, nine of us gather in a circle. As the women tell their stories, the room fills with agitation. Marianne is preparing to move to transitional housing. Starr's dog has just died. Cherry, who lives in her car, had lost her house because of legal costs to help her daughter and grandson. Varonne had lost both her parents when she was young. And there is Jen, part Cherokee and Cree, who had been orphaned at an early age.

Jen begins to spill out her life, but I realize that the focus needs to return to the circle. These women's problems are personal, but also part of a larger change taking place. I speak about women around the world, saying that there is a global crisis and that fragmentation is everywhere. I notice tears in the eyes of some of the women.

Ginny, who is co-facilitating this day, says, "My Zen teacher told me that the qualities that women have—love, compassion—are qualities that the world needs, but that women don't trust them so we don't manifest these qualities in our lives. He asked me to sit with women, to help them realize these qualities."

We then speak about homelessness, and one of the women says there is an inner home as well.

When we meditate, I can hear a woman crying. It is Jen. Afterwards she says, "I always knew of a girl who was whole. In meditation the girl returned, and this gives me comfort."

Reflection

What happened for Jen is something I've seen happen to other women. It is as if a reconnection takes place. A linking up inside of a woman, to an inner home. Each of us, in our own way, has a longing for this home (although we may call it something else), and sitting together in circles like this heals us all.

During meditation that day, Ginny had a vision. She told us, "I saw the 'grandmothers.' It was an image of grandmothers from many indigenous traditions." The atmosphere in the room as she spoke was peaceful and at ease. The women shared that the circle had helped them. How it gave them better focus, and more of a sense of calm. We gave each of them a gift of my book, *Women, Wisdom & Dreams,* and closed with a minute of silence.

Afterwards, Ginny and I stood outside on the sidewalk and talked. She explained, "When I saw the grandmothers, I prayed, 'Help your daughters.' And then they said, 'We can heal the women.'" Ginny and I saw this—how the women, as they left after the meeting, had a brightness in their eyes and talked animatedly with one another.

LONGING

Once there was a girl. There was no place for her natural, sacred self in her culture.

— KATHLEEN, in a writing practice that begins
with "Once there was a girl…"

A WOMAN'S GOLD

SARA WEARS MODEST, long skirts. Shining hair, light brown with gray streaks, falls down her back. There is a freshness, an impeccability about her, as if years of working as a nurse have become part of her nature. An injury had caused her to leave work and go onto disability.

Sara lives in her car, which has been her home for the last two years. She comes to our meetings and seems eager to be there. I don't know much about her past, until this one day as we are talking about a woman's wisdom, Sara speaks about her family.

My ancestors came over from England on the tall ships. One of the women was on the Mayflower. They were midwives and wise women, but often had to hide their knowledge.

The women grow quiet. There is a feeling in the air of something lost or, perhaps, just forgotten. Until now, I have held back details about my own life. But in this moment, it feels like time to share.

"Many years ago," I said, "Life was very difficult for me. People saw my outer persona, and I looked like a capable mother of young children. But when no one was around, I cried. I didn't even know why. It was like having tears behind my eyes, out of sight. But during this time I learned that my life wasn't a failure. I realized that I had a purpose, even in the difficulty. That's when I began to have dreams."

I told the women of a dream that changed my perspective. In the dream I see a man without a face. Only his eyes are visible, looking into my own. He tells me, "What you think of as depression, is longing. *I have loved you since before time. I have loved you always.*"

"That was when," I say to the women, "I discovered the power of longing."

The women listen. I note a feeling of relaxation in the room, and I can hear some of the women exhaling, like a deep sigh. It is as if every woman in the room has experienced that inner sorrow, but has never had a context for it. This kind of longing is not spoken of in our culture. There is little understanding of the nature of longing.

There is a moment of stillness, like when the wind drops. And then the women begin to talk about loss. They speak of the passing of a mother, a husband, a child, a house. And from there, their conversation digresses and loses focus. I just listen. It is a kind of listening that witnesses the women without judgment.

Sara turns to look at me. "What do you have to say about this?" she asks.

"What I have to say is this," I say. But it's a stalling tactic. I feel emptied of thought. A few moments later, a tingling sensation arises. The words come. I say, "I bow to the longing inside each of you."

Sara's eyes widen. "You *honor* us? No one has *ever* honored this. I thought I was crazy!"

We end with a minute of silence. All of our losses are held in peace.

Reflection

I have heard these words—*I thought I was crazy*—from so many women. An older, inner knowing is felt as something wrong. We don't recognize the value of our longing, how it nourishes, how it draws us closer to the heart of our being.

Months later, after Sara stopped coming to the circle because she found a place to live other than her car, I saw her when I was on a tour of county agencies. She was sitting in front of a computer when I walked into the room. "Sara?" I said. She turned around and then stood up and we embraced.

She was doing well, she said. And she thanked me for the gold. I was puzzled.

"*You know*," she said. "The gold you talked about in the meetings. You said how a woman is like gold, that she's always pure no matter what's happened to her. I use this every day, many times a day. I just remember the gold and then I have strength to do what I need to do. It helped me so many times."

A woman is like gold, she is like the Earth. She is never impure...the Earth purifies everything...the Earth is always pure.

—RADHA MOHAN LAL, 20th-century Sufi master

THE SINGING BIRD

WE SAT IN A CIRCLE AGAIN, in the room at the shelter where we meet. The beige blinds are down, but we can see, and hear, the children in the playground. It was not easy to listen to the women that day. Sometimes all we can do is listen, and inwardly hold them all in a loving way.

One young woman, striving to free herself from a complex family dynamic, told about her life—full of difficulties and losses. I listened intently. As she shared her pain, a bird flew towards the window. I couldn't see the actual bird, only its shadow through the screen. It was hopping on a branch, singing, hopping again.

I kept being drawn to the bird. It flitted and hopped around, as all the while the young woman talked of her troubles. Her life's sorrows were somehow joined by the tenderness of this bird. I thought of how sometimes the notion of longing is imaged as a bird, whose song is the soul's remembrance of wholeness.

Then, one of the other women in the circle noticed the little bird. There was her sorrow, and also this burst of birdsong. The young woman stopped talking. She thanked the women for listening. She didn't understand why all these feelings were coming up. "But now," she said, "I feel lighter."

We had a brief silent meditation. During this time, one of the women had a vision. She shared it after we meditated. "I saw a huge heart that held all of us in the circle, healing all." Longing is sometimes referred to as the feminine, or receptive side of love. It seemed to me that somehow that morning, we were all touched by this quality.

AN INNER CRY

THE FOLLOWING WEEK, along with Sara, come several new women. The theme of loss continues as the women share during their introductions. Around the circle the talking stone is passed. A woman will hold it, look at the stone, and then begin, finding her way through a labyrinth of feeling to words that might clarify her life.

When the talking stone comes to Sadie, she removes her sunglasses. Sadie is Haitian, but has lived in California for the last ten years. She carries a refined elegance, and an aura of sadness. Since coming to the circle, she has started to remember her dreams. Today, I learn the cause of her sorrow. But I also hear a deeper quality that, perhaps for the first time, is becoming conscious. She tells us her dream.

> *I was with a man. I don't know who he was. And he kissed me on the top of my head. I felt the greatest peace. Five years ago I lost my husband. I became depressed and this was the first time I felt this tenderness again. It gives me hope.*

In response, I describe how, years ago, I had no idea what longing was. I didn't know it existed. I learned that longing was how women connect to life and to the sacred within life.

All the while, on this day, a woman who seems to be in her early forties sits quietly next to me. It's her first time to the circle. She comes from Lake County, an hour north. Towards the end of the circle, there is a new and vibrant warmth and aliveness in her eyes. She says,

This has helped me today. When my Nana died, I lost myself. Nana cared for me when I was young. She helped me get on my feet to teach piano, which is what I used to do. It was because of her that I became an accomplished pianist. But after she died the family rejected me. I began to have migraines, but the doctors never found anything wrong. I'm healthy today, but a part of me disappeared when she died. I was looking everywhere, and didn't know this was it.

You've made me so happy. I came here three days ago with no hope. Everything was gone. But now I have hope. I'm intelligent and have skills. I want to know how to live this! It's real.

Reflection

The women who come to our circles readily embrace feminine values. I had imagined that there would be more resistance, which is why at first I didn't use words like longing, or the feminine. But gradually, I responded to the women's longing by giving it a framework. A name. This was freeing for the women, and also, for me personally.

Soon after, I no longer needed to address the feminine in this way. It had become part of the circle, a thread that ran through all of our meetings. Unspoken, yet affirmed.

I recall a woman, Kathleen who came to our meetings for several months. One day, she shared with the circle of women. She spoke spontaneously, as if, through her words, a conscious connection to life was being restored.

> *I was divorced after twenty-five years, was a soccer mom, did playgroups, but I never felt a deeper connection. Being in a shelter, I am finding out about women. About being connected in a genuine way. This is real feminine power. Having become friends with women in shelters, I feel how much we are connected.*
>
> *All the material things have been left behind. I never understood when women would say, "How can you let him talk to you like that?" I would think, "like what?" Even though inside I would feel terrible. I lost my house, cars, travel, prestige. But I've learned about the feminine.*

I see, again and again, that these circles are rooted in trust, grounded in love. And this allows women to feel their own dignity, which is a power in itself.

HOLDING SILENCE

Those of us in the shelter need a way to feed heart and soul. That's what we need.

—SANDY, who cared for her aging parents until
they died, and afterwards became homeless

⤜⤙

I understood from the group how to find a place of calm. When I'm in the shelter at night, and there's a lot of noise, I close my eyes and find this place in my heart, and can listen to my dreams and visions. Then I can find peace, and then I know what to do next. I need now to heal and also to train for community work.

—AVA, homeless for two months

THE WAY SILENCE ARISES

TODAY I FOUND MYSELF wishing I were anywhere else but here, sitting with the women. This feeling of wanting to turn away from their suffering was new to me. I observed it without judgment, curious as to what the feeling meant, and then it changed and dissolved like a cloud.

Around the room the women tell stories of what seem to be insurmountable difficulties. After the last woman speaks, the room falls into an uneasy silence. A few women close their eyes. They have grown accustomed to the way silence arises in the circle, creating a space held with love—a space to breathe and to simply be. I lead the women in a brief meditation, which I close a little more than five minutes later.

After the meditation, I remain quiet. Inwardly I ask to be able to hold the sorrow of the women in my heart. Two minutes go by, and still, there is silence. But there is a different quality now, a softening, like waves rising and falling.

One of the women breaks the silence and says that she feels calm. Another woman shares her experience of the meditation. One by one, they speak, and I realize that something is taking place at an inner level in the circle. I reach for my notebook and write down what the women are saying.

I feel steadier. Almost anchored.

I saw the wind, sweeping across fields, like wind on the wheat fields where I come from. I felt uplifted. It felt like I was at the ocean. I love to listen to the ocean and to feel its power. It connects me to God. Such beauty.

I like coming here. It makes me feel calm. I'm not anxious when I come here.

The women all look so relaxed, and in a certain way, their faces reveal a sweetness that comes with this kind of quietness. All this takes time, and allowing, although we haven't done very much. There are only ten minutes left in our circle. I ask the women for a word that expresses the feeling or quality they have now. Each offers their 'word,' but it is not so much an intellectual exercise as a recognition of what lives inside.

Knowledge

Listening

Compassion

Anxiety

Love

Peace

Healing

I realize that quiet and rest is where my intuition comes from.

I saw a landscape. And each hill is an obstacle I need to overcome. But I could see it from a calm place.

There is a quiet, mysterious place that can be found in the silence. Here we include rather than deny our fears, anxiety, or sorrow. And then in this interior place something is done, a work invisible to the eye but recognized by the heart. This is not a matter of learning. It is a remembering.

A QUIET SPACE

THERE IS A POWER in the quiet. The women know this, which is why they come. They may not speak of it as the feminine, but they carry this understanding. One of the women who arrived at the circle one day sat down with an anxious expression on her face. Pat is in her late sixties, older than many of the other women who have come to the circle.

She speaks clearly, articulately, and with humility. These are the traits that stand out whenever she has shared in the circle. Pat has been without a home a year and a half, and professes that she never expected to find herself living in a shelter.

During the introductions the first time she came, she said, "I just want to sit with you all in a quiet space." Four months later, Pat has been present nearly every week and expresses her appreciation.

> *I always walk out of here with more strength than when I walked in. You create a space here, and we can get in touch with our feelings and what's inside us. You offer the space and we do what we want with the space. It's up to us.*

At the circle that day Pat says several times that a social worker has told her she would soon have a place. I feel she is trying to convince herself of this, so after the circle is over, I say that it takes courage to trust that she'll find housing. She shakes her head. "It's not courage. I just do what's next. I have to, or else I'd never get out of homelessness."

A few weeks later, Pat told me that she had moved into an apartment. She would be able to live there for years. I thought that was the last time I would see her, but she continues to come to the circle with the permission of the shelter. Living alone was not as easy as she imagined. Feelings that had been pushed aside during the last year and a half now surfaced. She needed, and longed, to sit together with other women in a sacred way. The shelter hired her as an intern to help other women who are newcomers, so she was able to continue to join the circle.

Reflection

I thought about the isolation and loneliness that Pat experienced once she moved away from the shelter, because at the same time, another woman in the circle also found an apartment and asked if she too could continue attending. I saw that the silence held in the circle serves as a connector— a bridge—that strengthens the capacity of women to live on their own.

FINDING THE SELF

I WAS DRAWN to the work of youth worker and community activist Orland Bishop from the first time I heard a talk of his on the Internet. He spoke with a depth and wisdom that seemed to permeate the thick walls of our divided society, giving me hope and inspiration for the circles with homeless women.

The founder and director of ShadeTree Multicultural Foundation, Orland works with inner city youth in Los Angeles and speaks around the world. I met him almost by accident at a memorial, standing outside on a bright, gusty afternoon near the San Francisco Bay. Orland carries a marked nobility—a regal quality—although he came from a humble background in Africa. I recognized him and, knowing that I might not have another opportunity to talk with him, introduced myself. He recalled a mutual friend who had mentioned me to him.

Then something interesting happened. He asked, "What is your work?" I told him about the circles with newly homeless women. Orland touched his chest and made a slight bow. He was completely present even though there were several hundred people in the room. "Thank you," he said. In that moment he spoke to my soul, not to my persona or to anything I did.

In my vulnerability from being seen so deeply, I stumbled to reply, but I asked him what I wanted to ask. "How do you create a space for such transformations among marginalized youth, and how do you create a truce in gangs? How do you do it? Could we talk about this sometime?"

"Call me anytime," he said.

A few weeks later, I did call him, and he answered while waiting for his flight at an airport. I asked two questions. Could he describe more fully this space he creates for the troubled youth? And how does it work? "Yes," he said. After a brief silence, he continued the conversation we had begun a few weeks ago.

As he spoke, Orland's answers seemed to rise from ancient wisdom, like stars that carry light from long ago.

Attention is what the infant human being needs in the world. Everything begins there, as a way of touch. Most people are looking for that encounter. To refrain from judgment with another.

In the Christian tradition, it is said: "Lest we become like a child, we cannot enter the kingdom of heaven." Only if we can see the human being as a child in this way, otherwise we cannot enter their life.

The child is an inner space, with all the potential to heal, to begin, to inspire. We hold that for them. These refined qualities we hold, and this begins a dialogue. Even if we sit in silence, there too is a dialogue.

Our particular task is to make sure we can find what we are looking for: the Self. The Self is the will to become. Each person needs to find this capacity of knowing how to become. For some people it comes through difficult experiences. For others, it comes through privilege. We hold that for another.

Reflection

Holding. This is not an easy concept in our collective understanding. We may hold a dream that comes at night. The next morning we might not understand it, but it has startled us awake. It has meaning that will unfold only over time. This is how we hold a dream.

But to hold a difficulty, to sit silently with it, and not to prematurely 'fix' it, this is something else. Like carrying a child in the womb, in the darkness. We sing to the child, but she or he remains hidden. This knowledge of holding new life is in women's bodies whether or not we ever have children. We can do this for one another.

One day a woman came to the circle, and said, "Is this one of those places where we have to be positive? And everything we say has to be upbeat? Because that just didn't work."

"No," I said. "This isn't one of those places. You just need to be yourself."

She paused, and said she'd stay.

Later, after the meditation, she spoke first. "I've had so much stress. But it started to move down from my head. I could feel it move down my body, to my feet. And then the stress just left. I was able to cry for the first time in a year."

A HEALING DREAM

VANESSA DIDN'T SPEAK the first month she came to our circles. She sat hunched forward, her blond hair skimming the middle of her back, her legs crossed at the knee. She always wore fitted jeans with a stylish jacket. I knew only that she was a student at the junior college.

When I saw her outside in the courtyard, she always gave me a bright smile and said that she was fine, but behind her eyes I sensed a deep sorrow. Sometimes Vanessa cried during meditation.

Then, one day she spoke. Her boyfriend is ill. Her young daughter lived with them in a small apartment but they could no longer pay for rent, and went to a shelter. Seeing him in pain is too much to bear.

Over the year, Vanessa came often to our weekly circles. Sometimes we wouldn't see her for weeks, but then she would appear again. Each time she came, she would talk more easily, sharing more about her life, but still deeply troubled.

Vanessa walked into the room where we hold the circle, and before we even started, said that she had a dream. She never had a dream like this before, she said.

I saw an Asian woman and she was so kind. She gave me a glass of water. I've never tasted anything like it. It tasted so sweet and good. I drank the water and felt purified. There was a pink lychee

floating in the water. It was sweet too. I feel like
I've been washed clean!

I don't know what caused Vanessa to feel impure.

But now, while telling the dream, Vanessa is shining. She sat up straight, her shoulders back. I sensed that whatever had caused her to feel impure, was gone.

We didn't see Vanessa for another month. But then she came in to tell us that her boyfriend's mother had offered them a place to live. She would stay to finish her semester, and then move to Iowa where her boyfriend could heal, and her daughter would be cared for in a home environment.

Vanessa's dream, with images of pure water and a pink lychee, has to do with love and grace. The water signifies the receptive quality of the feminine, the sacred that exists in Vanessa, that we as witnesses to her dream could hold.

This is what we do. We hold an empty space for the women so that they can receive the answers for themselves.

CONNECTION

I felt my feet on the ground. I felt my heart beating. I felt connected to something, I was a part of it.

—JASMINE, homeless for six months,
after her first time meditating

〉〉〉《《《

I felt connected, effortlessly. Silence brought me energy.

—MONICA, junior college student,
homeless for five months

THIS PURE PLACE

NESTLED IN A GROVE of redwood trees on the outskirts of town, Taylor House is a protected, residential shelter for women. Standing outside, I hear a hawk's cry, and a creek's soft rippling. Although time and again I've seen the value these circles have for women, my old doubts arise for a moment. I wonder if these circles truly do help the women. I pray to be empty, ask to be aligned inwardly.

I am here because of Trina, who attended our circle in another shelter for nearly a year and has lived here for the last five months. Of Native American and Japanese descent, she is a natural leader among the women. Like a shepherd, she watches out for those around her. She said to the women here, "Come to the circle. It will help you. It helped me."

It took four months to go through the finger printing and background checks required for us to start the group. Finally, we are here. As it's a new program, we will be observed by a staff member. When Trina asked Ginny and me to offer our circles here, I wondered if it would work with such a small shelter—housing just twenty-four women. Taylor House offers counseling to help the women get on their feet and find jobs. Since most of them are at work today, fewer than ten will be in our circle.

As I enter the building, I smell a tangy cleanliness, as if the floors are washed daily with bleach. The caseworker on duty is talking on the phone and waves me through to the sitting room where the circle will take place. It is an area by the kitchen, with two sofas and chairs that form a circle around a coffee table.

I light a candle and sit, waiting. A few minutes later, two women walk in, and then another woman with Trina. Ginny arrives a few minutes late, carrying pink dahlias from her garden and shells, which she arranges on the coffee table in the middle of the circle. Then the caseworker silently takes her place on the sofa.

I feel calmer than I did when I first arrived, but my earlier doubts still nag at me, and Trina, always cheerful, appears to be struggling with something too. She sits upright, her face tense. She doesn't look at me as I introduce Ginny and myself. I continue with asking the women for introductions and a brief description of what they are hoping for today, going clockwise around the circle. Like the other women, Trina simply says her name.

In spite of the windows being open to the cool morning air, there feels to be no opening in the room, only an unspoken tension. I am aware of being visible to these women, as they are to me. They are sensitive to feeling, to mood, for they have been through crises where they needed to develop a deep awareness for others. I haven't encountered this wall of resistance in any other shelter. I address this by immediately beginning our meditation. Outside, a branch rubs against another tree. A bird chirps. Inside the room, there is deep silence.

As I try to meditate, I am floundering. How to proceed? I decide to share about my life after the meditation is complete. This is not what I normally do in the beginning of a new program.

Twenty-five years ago, I was sitting quietly, meditating for the first time. After a few minutes, I inwardly saw an image of a starving girl. I could barely look at her. I felt repulsion. A friend with more experience suggested I try to touch her, fingertip to fingertip. But I couldn't. For the next few weeks after this, I took a walk in the early mornings when my family was still asleep, and returned to this image of the girl.

One day I put her in my heart. Something happened, and I began to cry. I asked the girl who she was, and why she had appeared. I heard, in the wordless ways of the inner world, that she was here to help me. She knows joy, and can help in decisions. She needs my attention.

The image never returned. I later learned that there is a place in a woman that is always whole. Like gold, it can never be violated.

After a brief meditation, I pass around paper and pens. I tell the women, if you'd like to write, then begin with *Once there was a girl…* Write freely, and see what comes.

As the women focus on writing, the opening I'd been missing enters with a breeze of fresh air. Something is happening. Eight minutes pass, and the wall is crumbling.

I ask the women to wrap up their writing. One of the younger women, who in the beginning of the circle had only stared out the window, asks if she can read first.

Once there was a girl who lived in the woods. No connection to the outside world, everything was pure and untouched. She did not understand the harsh realities of the real world, fear, anger, loneliness...she only understood love. She loved the animals of the woods and they loved her. She took care of the animals, and they took care of her. The streams took care of her, with fresh water. The trees took care of her, giving shelter. She understood survival from bigger predators in the forest. She understood there was a cycle in life, everything began, lived, and died, giving back to the earth, starting over again.

She's elated. "I didn't know I could write!" We listen. One of the women whispers, "Beautiful."

Other women read too, and the stories uncover a hidden wisdom. The women listen attentively to each other. The relaxation that occurs during the circle, especially in the reading of their stories and writing, brings ease that dispels the earlier tensions, and allows the women to experience their connection to life.

Trina starts to speak. She looks at me, and I can see how her face has softened, and her eyes have the usual spark that I noticed before in her.

I feel so relaxed now. When you said that this pure place gets covered over, I realize that I've known this, then forgotten it. We need it to survive, such

as getting work, housing. It's underneath every-
thing we do, and it makes life easier. It's the pure
place—the spiritual ground—that's underneath
everything. I just need to come from my heart,
and then my life makes sense.

The six of us close our eyes for another brief meditation of the heart. I enter a deep state and see an image—six potted plants with tiny, deep blue flowers, in a circle.

I open my eyes and behold the circled women. Their devotion is ready to be planted into the earth. I want to say something, but I don't want to disturb this sweet silence. And then, the social worker speaks, for the first time. She explains that she wants to share her experience while meditating in the circle.

I saw a shaft of gold wheat. Just pure gold.

The women's faces show wonder and, for some, joy. I ask if she understands the meaning of the image. *Yes*, she says. We sit in silence for a few moments. I am aware of how the circle holds the women, equally. And then she speaks.

She says that many years ago she was homeless. In the last five years, she has lost four loved ones. But now, a shaft of gold wheat has risen up from her depths.

She wants no explanation or interpretation. Her face softens as this pure essence fills her.

The woman next to her, an assistant to the caseworker, nods her head in agreement. All the women read and listen intently, the stories uncovering an undiscovered wisdom, opening them to their own beauty and purity.

Now peace has settled over the circle. We sit in silence for the last two minutes. I sense we are each feeling our connection to our own inner 'gold.' No one wants to get up, so we talk until the women leave for community work in town.

Ginny leaves to teach a dance class in a nearby city. I get into my car, still feeling the amazed sense of wonder at the transformation that occurred during this meeting. Driving down the road shaded by towering eucalyptus trees, I miss my turn. I realize that I was in a deep state and pull over to drink some water before continuing home.

Reflection

There are some meetings, like this one, that stay with me as vividly as the day they happened. These times of intimacy seem to affect life itself. Not just the women sitting in the circle, but permeating down to a deeper layer of life. They touch in the same way that sunlight warms a cold rock. Or how a pinch of salt flavors an entire soup. We are all connected parts of life, and so what happens to one part also touches the whole. This speaks of a collective story deeper than our mind's comprehension. Grace is present, speaking a language known to the heart.

YOU KNOW WHO I AM

PAIGE STOOD in the main room of the day shelter. Women were talking all around her, sitting at long tables, and she looked lost. I asked, "Would you like to come to our women's circle? It starts in ten minutes." She smiled shyly and shook her head, saying that she didn't speak English well enough. I told her that it didn't matter, and that she could come anyway. So she did.

In the circle, Paige said only that she was from Micronesia, and that she couldn't speak. But something happened when the circle was over. The women left, all but Paige. She had a sturdy physique, and appeared to have a sweetness that lacked discernment. Paige walked over to me and asked if we could talk. I invited her to sit down next to me, on the gray plastic chairs we use for the circle.

"What do you want?" she asked softly.

"Nothing," I said.

She asked again, "What do you *want*?"

Her question startled me. I knew I had to answer her question honestly.

"You have a good heart, a pure heart," I said. "Please take care of it. This isn't an easy culture to live in."

Tears came to her eyes, and I knew that she understood what I was saying.

The next week, she came again to the circle. After we meditated, I suggested a writing exercise. But Ginny said quietly to me that one of the women from Mexico couldn't write. I quickly added that the women could draw instead of writing.

The women worked quietly for seven minutes, and I asked if anyone wanted to share. Paige smiled shyly and held up a pencil drawing of a dolphin's tail rising up out of the ocean. It filled the page. On the top margin, she had written *Dolphin's Tale*. Her voice, with the softest trace of an accent like the ocean she described, came alive as she spoke.

Paige told us how she used to swim with the dolphins every day, how they made her happy. Now in America she needs work so that she can send money to her family. She misses her family, she said, and the dolphins.

A woman who sat next to Paige opened her eyes wide. She said, "People in this country pay a ton of money to swim with the dolphins. And you got to swim with them every day?" There was laughter in the circle, and Paige was surrounded by warmth. She tilted her head shyly and smiled.

The third week Paige came to the circle, she didn't give her name. Instead, she looked at me. "*You know who I am*," she said. With a strength in her voice that I hadn't heard before, she spoke about how she had left a difficult relationship, and found a house and a new job.

When Paige was leaving after the circle ended, she turned at the door and again looked at me. Like a refrain, she said, "You know who I am." She paused. "Thank you for welcoming me."

Reflection

This welcoming that we do in circles seems a simple gesture, but it is essential for healing the social fabric of life. The women hunger for connection with their forgotten places, their souls. Through the circles, we make connection within our own inner lives and with the network of relationships around us, as well as the greater web of life.

TIME TO BREATHE

LIAT WAS FIFTEEN minutes late. We were just beginning to meditate when she walked into the room. I noticed the solidity of the way she held herself. She had a sense of harmony in the quiet way she found a chair, and sat without disturbing the circle. I explained the meditation and the room fell into silence.

Later, we went around the room, the women speaking about their experience of the silence. Liat spoke freely.

After fourteen years of living with my partner, he kicked me out. I'm seeing an attorney, a man who is impartial with great skills. I am learning to trust again. I told him that.

I went to the job center the other day and a woman drove me back. I was grateful to her and told her so. The woman said that her son tells her that everyone has a purpose. That every breath is given because God wants you to have that breath. So to be grateful for every breath. That's what we forget. I've learned so much.

I told the woman in the shelter here that I have to find a job, so why would I want to go to a meeting with meditation? But then I realized I needed to be here. So thank you. I come from a spiritual family and know this is so important. We

*have time for TV and computers but who has time
for their own breath? That is what I needed today.
To breathe.*

*I tell some friends of my difficulties. The next
time they see me they say, "What are you doing
about the problem in your life?" I say, "I don't have
a problem. I have a difficulty and a challenge."*

*I am a childhood educator. One day a little
girl came to me with a difficult story about her
life. I reached into two invisible pockets and said,
"I have a key in each pocket. One key is for a happy life. The other is for a miserable life. Which key
do you choose?" The little girl asked for the happy
key. Ten minutes later the rest of the kids came in,
and said they wanted a happy key too.*

Two weeks later, Liat was sitting at a table in the main
room at the shelter, confident that she would be leaving.
She had received money to help her with housing and
would go back to work.

There was something rare about Liat in how she could
connect with and speak from her own clarity and focus. She
touched the other women, like a light that shows the way.

RECLAIMING WHAT IS HIDDEN

WHAT I HAVE WITNESSED among the women in our circles is a deep and profound connection with life that surfaces into consciousness. Given the space, the silence, the listening, and the welcoming, the essence of a woman emerges, through story, image, or feeling. And this always reconnects a woman to her relationship with life.

I remember how Melanie came to the circle—only once. Something happened that day. She sat down next to me, head bowed, hair covering part of her face. She could have been the age of my own daughters, somewhere in her early thirties. She did not speak at all, except to state her name during the introductions.

Following a short meditation I suggest a writing exercise to begin with the words, "Once there was a seed." Don't judge what you write, I say to the women. Just let a story be told.

For the next five minutes, everyone is focused on their writing. When the time is up, several of the women read aloud. For some reason I didn't expect Melanie to share her writing. Maybe it was because she was so scrunched up inside herself, so weary. But without looking up, she starts to read. She reads quickly, so I ask her to read it again, but a little slower so we can hear her more clearly. And she readily agrees. At this point, Melanie has looked up, suddenly present with us. There is an aliveness in her eyes, which wasn't there when she first sat down. Her voice changes as she reads in a more measured, confident way.

Once there was a seed. A seed that by no stretch of the imagination could have grown. It did not have the right circumstances to grow—no water, no food. But the light came and touched the seed, and in the warmth, it grew up to the light. It should not have been possible. But it grew!

This moment felt like pure magic. Not the kind where one tries to influence another through one's own actions or words, but the simple wonder of life emerging on its own. It was as if life could now flow through Melanie, whereas before she had been caught in impossibility and hopelessness. Quiet fills the circle, and with it comes a feeling of peace. Melanie looks around the room, and speaks freely. "I'm a single mother of a seven-year-old son. This is my first day of being homeless. I lost a job, then a home."

She then pauses, and says that she knows what she needs to do now. We witness this little transformation, acknowledging it simply by our attention, and listening with our heart.

In a few weeks Melanie no longer needs the services of the shelter. Was this grace? Or a combination of factors giving her a new framework from which she could draw on inner strength?

We see this again and again in the circles. When a woman remembers who she is, even for a moment, this

provides her with the foundation from which to partici-
pate more deeply in life. She moves from feeling frag-
mented and isolated to flowing fully with the stream of life.

BEAUTY

Once there was a flower that smelled good and the flower was as pure as a snowflake with the buds all around the stem. It didn't look real at all, but as you walked by the flower you got a good smell so you knew it was real. I really wanted to pick it but I left it alone so everybody could see and feel and smell the scent of the beautiful flower.

—JOANNA, during the writing practice

ONCE THERE WAS A FLOWER

I PASS AROUND a box of cards with stunning photographs of morning glories to the eight women who've come to the circle today. "Choose one that you like, and then we'll write on the cards," I say. I explain that it's an exercise to help access our deeper knowing about who we are, and about life.

A young mother chooses a blue morning glory that is surrounded by darkness. She says, "I like the light and the dark. It reminds me I have this light inside."

I suggest they begin with the words *Once there was a flower...* and write freely. The women write, and their concentration seems to relax them. After five minutes, I invite anyone to read aloud what they wrote.

Irma, who rarely talks in the circle, then speaks. She came from South America ten years ago. Her soft yet sturdy voice, laced with the accent of her birthplace, is almost musical. It draws me in.

She begins by saying that she reacted with anger towards someone at the shelter. She realized that she lost compassion for that person. Her writing, she says, follows that experience. I wonder if the writing is a vehicle for her to communicate what she might not want to say in front of others, who are now listening attentively.

Once there was a flower, this flower called morning glory. It has a beautiful energy. A white light is in the center. Also in the center there is a color yellow or gold which is the color of wisdom, or the divine. The petals are blue, which is the color of protection, power, and strength. This morning glory flower makes me feel that I have the wisdom in the center of myself, the power, the protection, which surrounds me so I can do the things I need to do. I just need to know that I have the wisdom within me. The power and strength to keep going, to sing my glory.

A PERFUME WHOSE
ESSENCE IS NOT LOST

DURING A RADIO SHOW, an interviewer asked about my work with homeless women. During the call-in questions after the interview, one of the listeners said that she worked as an advocate for homeless women in Olympia, Washington. She then told a dream:

> *I am at a high, holy celebration in a synagogue—*
> *a feast, with a long banquet table set up, eating*
> *a special meal. I have trouble finding my place.*
> *I feel really out of place. I wander into another*
> *room, and there are rows and rows of glass shelves,*
> *with perfume bottles. Many are very old. Inside is*
> *a beautiful, gold amber liquid.*
>
> > *I breathe in some of the wonderful fragrances.*
> *They were donated by a wealthy woman, and every-*
> *body gets to choose one. I think that when perfume*
> *gets very old, that the fragrance would go bad. But*
> *I am told: "This perfume never loses its essence."*

Perfume has to do with the essence—the beauty—of a woman. This essential beauty nourishes life. From this woman's dream, I knew to pay particular attention to her because although she didn't yet understand the depth of her dream, I sensed she would be able to offer to other women a reflection of their own real nature. We stayed in touch.

In a phone conversation several months later, she said that our conversations helped her to envision creating programs for women that would nourish them spiritually, as well as provide for their daily needs. This was her intention, to work with women spiritually, but she didn't know how this could come about. Over the next few months, she was invited to be a part of a working group in her city that was creating the first permanent residential shelter for the homeless. She began to offer circles for women, but felt a constraint in how she ran them. Then she had a dream showing her a different way to work, and emailed me about it.

In my dream, I am working very hard at my advocacy job but don't feel like my efforts are resulting in getting enough folks placed in housing, even though everybody is saying we are doing a great job. I have a realization that the place to be really successful at housing folks is right next to where I am working...just a few steps from where I currently am. I can even see the spot...and I have the feeling that I am keeping the truth of this fact from myself and colluding with others to keep the truth hidden. The better place to be is a lighter color in my dream...like where I currently work is kind of grey and shadowy and where the successful work is being done has a soft, warm pink light emanating from it. This, I realize, is the feminine way.

I responded to her dream:

> There's a part of us that always tries to keep the truth of ourselves hidden. But there's no turning away from it now, because you know this place exists. And it's so close to you that you could even see it.
>
> The dream speaks of how a different quality of consciousness is needed in order to be more 'successful.' This different quality has to do with love. That's the light and warmth of the pink colored place.
>
> So there are several ways to work, as you were shown in the dream. One that seems outwardly successful, more visible to others, and another, more invisible way that touches a woman in the core of her being.
>
> When I hold a circle, I hold each woman's heart in my own when we begin. I've never spoken about it, but I recently found out that the other co-facilitators intuitively do this too. We hold them with love. This warmth is what's needed. Your dream is showing you this very real need, and that you can meet it by stepping into this new office.

Reflection

I was struck by the beauty in both of this woman's dream images—first through the scent or perfume, and then through the color. Beauty is the language of the feminine, of the soul, which most women innately understand.

Seemingly by chance, she happened to join the teleconference, and then shared her dream. But life's connections are an aspect of the sacred feminine. Once we offer ourselves in service to life, even without knowing what that means, life tends to take us where we are needed. This too is the hand of beauty.

GLORY

SHE WEARS A DENIM jacket with a bright blue t-shirt. There's a hardiness about her, like a plant that survives a severe winter. The only reason she came, she says, is because her friend asked her. She is in her mid-forties.

She doesn't speak except to tell us her name, Vivienne, and that she's Native American. No one else wants to talk so I suggest we meditate and then have a writing exercise. They can begin with *"Once there was a woman…"* Vivienne is the first to offer to read aloud.

> *Once there was a woman coming down off a mountain. As she came closer to me I could see a flock of birds flying above her head. They were small birds, hummingbirds, and seemed to be almost standing still around her head, like a crown or halo. She was very beautiful. Soon she was standing in front of me. She was looking me in the eyes and said one word, and then she was gone. "Glory."*

I never saw Vivienne at the shelter again. She was just passing through, accompanying her friend. But she left her story, of the beautiful bird woman. Sometimes these stories carry blessings not just for the woman herself, but for all of us.

ONE DAY WE DANCED

THERE WE WERE, eight women standing in a circle in the middle of the room, holding hands. Earlier, I'd felt agitation within the group and a sense of hopelessness among some of the women. I wasn't in a particularly good mood myself and had low expectations for this session. But during the time for sharing, Ginny mentioned the power of dance, and how in ancient times, dancing in a circle had been like prayer for women. It was how they connected to the divine. But that over time this had been suppressed by a patriarchal culture.

This gave me the idea that we could dance. And after asking the women if they wanted to dance, we stood up. Ginny showed us a simple movement—one step right, another step to the right, then one to the left. She led us all moving in silence, and then one of the women began to hum a sweet refrain.

One woman—Lisa—had a hard time following. Grimacing, she struggled to find the rhythm. Another stumbled, but then was able to move in time with Ginny. In the silence, and then with the soft humming, I could feel a shift in the circle. The intense focus on their feet brought us all together in the present moment. We stepped joyfully.

After a few minutes the dancing slowed, and then we stood still. There was peacefulness among the women.

Lisa returned to her chair. Her worn face had softened.

Leaning back, she said, "Such beauty. I feel beauty inside me. I needed to know this."

Reflection

One day I spoke about the qualities of beauty to the women. I described beauty as a power that belongs to women but that isn't recognized. One of the women then described what happened when she brought beauty into the shelter. Her locker was situated by the water dispenser where people lingered as they filled their water bottles, or just came for a drink.

"I don't know why I did this," she explained, but she created a kind of altar on top of her locker with a cloth, some shells and rocks, and a flower when she could find one. It was appreciated by the people who began to spend more time there. They paused, and relaxed, taking time to connect to others drawn by beauty. One woman told her that seeing her locker each day made her happy. No one knew why, she said.

Experiences of beauty such as this woman's simple altar, or our little circle dance, serve to connect people to something inside themselves—to their innate power, sense of peace, and belonging. On some deep level, beauty is part of our notion of home. It helps ground us here, now, in the place where we are.

DEVOTION

Two nights ago, I dreamt that a hawk was trying to get into my heart, but I was afraid to let the hawk in.

—ALIYA, living in a homeless shelter for a year

⇛⇚

In my dream, I saw a man that I know. He was standing there and said, "I'm here for you. I've been waiting for you." He embraced me. It was a contact that I needed, that I wanted. It was very natural, very soft. With him I felt very safe. I've never had a dream like this before. Now I'm not afraid to listen to my dreams. Before, they were all bad. Now I have had other dreams, like this one. I carry the feeling. I hold the feeling of this dream.

— LUISA, homeless for four months, now working towards becoming a community social worker

LONG AGO, during a difficult time in my life, I became aware of denying myself a quality of devotion. I recognized that what was missing was the joy inside of life, the song inside of silence.

Devotion for a woman is like a sunflower turning to face the sun as it moves through the day. It's the part of us that is always attuned to the Source. For many of us, this natural relationship to life became hidden from our own consciousness. Over the centuries, women's powerful connection with the Sacred was obscured by shame, and devalued. Our culture does not reflect back to a woman her need for devotion.

Without devotion, the river of life does not flow. That was my experience of this powerful and innate quality that belongs to women. In our circles, I can share this with the women, not through anything I say, but simply through a way of being. Devotion is so intrinsic to a woman. Without this natural devotion, we are left dry, cut off from the sustenance of grace. In our circles, we simply acknowledge devotion. A door opens.

AN UNDISCOVERED LANDSCAPE

SEVERAL YEARS AGO, in a living room that looks out to the sparkling Mississippi River, I wonder how to articulate what I had in my mind to a Benedictine nun, who happens to also be a psychologist and Jungian analyst. I begin to explain my interest in the meaning of devotion in women's lives. She looks out the window, listening thoughtfully, but there is a sense of uneasiness, as if she doesn't want to speak about it. So I explain what devotion means to me. That it has to do with a relationship to the divine—and that this relationship holds all other relationships in life.

She nods, and the tension eases. I realize that for many women, this place has needed to be hidden and protected from misunderstanding or misuse. I ask her what had she learned about women, our culture, and its relationship to devotion. She answers, now speaking freely:

Devotion is a natural instinct, but it has been diverted. It is often seen as a weakness, and then there is a betrayal of this natural instinct. We have been warned against trusting ourselves.

There is a deep place in women, and that place is sealed off. It is viewed with suspicion. Women forget themselves. They struggle against guilt. Women in particular are scared of boredom, of emptiness. They are frightened of being in

a space where nothing appears to be happening.
And so they forget the dearest things we have. It's
so important for women not to kill off what is dear
to us. Women struggle to value themselves.

I stop taking notes. I want to be more present, and to see her face as she speaks with such clarity. I had brought my audio recorder and now turn it on. She continues:

I see in women a fear of being quiet. There is a
space inside of them, and it is unknown, undis-
covered. People impose themselves on this space,
rather than trusting this sense of knowing, holding
the pieces, and listening. In the last ten to fifteen
years, I have seen how there are few maps for
Americans, few maps for their interior landscapes.
It is as if the inner world has often been turned
into a psychological concept.

But there is a great mystery to the soul. There
has been an attempt to soften this mystery, to
make it nice. But it can be fierce, unrelenting. In
those depths, there we find our devotion.

A SEED OF LOVE

TWO DAYS AFTER the tragic bombing at the Boston Marathon, a cloud of sorrow hangs over the circle of women who have come to the shelter. The program director tells me that the women are particularly in need of our circle today.

During the circle, the women, speaking of their sadness following the news, also told their own stories of neglect, of cruelty. I shifted in my seat. No matter how many times I've listened to similar stories, it doesn't get easier to hear them. But during meditation, as the women sat in silence, the feeling in the room lightened. And when the meditation ended, I asked, "If you had a seed that you could plant in your heart, what would it be?" One by one, going clockwise round the circle, each woman shared:

A seed of love.
A seed of light.
A seed of compassion.
A seed of love.
A seed of love.
A seed of inner peace.

And then Marisa spoke. Marisa had come to the circle for the last four months. Her mother is Mexican, her father Hungarian.

Something's always been missing. I didn't know what it was. But coming here is the first time I've gotten hold of it. It's like something that I needed but I didn't have a name for it.

It was my birthday yesterday. Every year my family forgets it. The day goes by and I think, well, nobody will remember. But this year my daughter brought a cake and all the kids celebrated. Even my boyfriend remembered. I think this has to do with how I've changed. Like something inside that touches outside.

Marisa teaches young women how to sew. She is also a grandmother, and has said openly that her purpose is to teach. Aside from teaching sewing, it is evident that she teaches a way of being to her grandchildren. At first she didn't say much, but she always expressed her appreciation of the circle at the end of our meeting. Her level of anxiety visibly decreased over this time. It was always a joy to see her. But I didn't realize just how much she had been touched by the circles.

Marisa shared how her life had begun to change, and soon she would no longer need the services of the shelter. But it seemed that her own devotion to life—to her grandchildren and the young women in Mexico—sometimes needed refreshment, like drinking a glass of clear water. So after that point, Marisa would periodically drop in to the circle for a few visits in a row.

Reflection

Marisa's sharing, and subsequent need to come back to the circle for periods to 'refresh,' showed me that, while a woman's devotion is a light that connects her to what is real and sustaining within, it cannot be isolated. We draw strength simply by being with each other, held and holding in this sacred way.

Working with the women for these last five years has brought insights about the nature of devotion that have touched my own life. One day I had a dream that helped me to understand why a woman's devotion serves the community around us.

> *A woman shows me a new water facility. I go inside and see that some men have recently constructed it. It is a large structure with a fresh, new feeling. The men have found a new source of water. Clear, clean water surges up from deep inside the earth. It bubbles up like water from a natural spring. There is so much water available. But then I am concerned. Will this dry up the groundwater? But the man reassures me that this water comes from an unending source. It is not finite and can't be exhausted.*

TENDING NEW LIFE

TARA PULLS HER CHAIR close to mine. I'm surprised to see her. Tara has a wildness to her that protects her, somehow. Her dark hair is loose around her shoulders, as if it's been blown by the wind. When I first met her, several years ago, I was struck by her raw honesty, at least with me.

Before we even begin the circle, Tara says that her grandma came to her in a dream. There's an urgency in her voice. I let her speak even though the circle has not begun. I know that Tara will leave almost immediately after sharing. She is unable to sit still.

Grandma gives me a baby. She tells me that I have to step up to the plate. I say I can't do this, I'm 40. I can't have a baby now. My grandma says it doesn't matter. I tell her that my old man is 59. She says it doesn't matter.

The dream scares me. I don't understand it. She told me that my life would change. And that I would start singing. They say my mom was a medicine woman.

My grandma is always trying to tell me things but I've been afraid, because of what happened when I was young, and my dream came true. My grandma says she'll be with me. She'll be by my side.

"What's it mean?" she asks. "Am I going to have a baby?"

I tell her that this is not a real baby, but a symbol of something new. Can she understand this? I ask. It's a potential in her. The dream is telling her that she needs to learn how to care for what is being born inside of her. "My grandma said she'd tell me how," says Tara.

I also say that this is a dream she can trust. Tara nods her head, her hands spread out on her thighs, as if to give her balance. This dream is a gift, I say. Tara, as always, gets up to leave. "I have to go," she says.

Over three years, my encounters with Tara were like this one. She would find me on Thursday morning, and before the circle, or afterwards, she would tell me a dream. "What's it mean?" she would ask.

In a minute or two, we would talk about it. Then she would leave. I saw changes in Tara over time. One day, a year ago, she was calmer, and she told me that she was in recovery. Her hair was combed, her clothes clean. She was not homeless, but at risk of homelessness. She lived at the edge, financially. The last time I saw her, she said, "Things are changing. I'm gonna be okay."

Will Tara be able to live her dream? A dream of new life that needs her attention, her care and devotion, and her willingness to trust the wisdom of her ancestors? I have not seen her in a year, which is usually a good indicator that she does not need services from the shelter.

MAKING A SHIFT

JENNIFER CAME ONLY ONCE. She wore silver brace-
lets, a denim jacket, and a pink t-shirt, and didn't say a
word, except during the introductions. "I'm here because
Celeste told me to come."

There she sat, during the circle, expressionless. Until
the writing exercise. And then she wrote eagerly, and was
the first to share when I invited the women to read aloud
what they wrote. Her voice was sturdy as she read:

> *Once there was a girl who, every day when she
> walked to school, passed a steep rocky cliff. She re-
> ally wanted to climb up that cliff but she knew she
> was too young and not strong enough. Years went
> by. She kept passing the cliff but knew she wasn't
> ready yet. Then, one day she passed the cliff and
> knew she was ready. She climbed the cliff.*

Every woman in the circle thanked her. Her face, previously impassive, lit up, and she looked surprised at the
response to her writing. We were all struck by the story's
power—by this tale of trusting the process of a woman's
transformation, sustained by her devotion to wholeness.
The process has its own rhythms and cycles, like the sea-
sons. It touches the same place again and again, until
something changes inside.

A LIGHT IN THE DARK

AT THE FIRST SESSION in a new shelter, seven women arrive to try our new program. Unfortunately, the chattering of volunteers comes through the moveable partition that was supposed to create privacy for our meeting.

After giving an introduction, I ask the women to tell their names and maybe, if they want to, to share briefly why they came to the circle. But they sit uneasily; each saying only her name.

When Ellen accepts the talking stone, she tells us she'd moved to the shelter three weeks ago. It was a necessity, she explains. That was all. The sounds of the cleanup crew continue. I suggest we start the meeting with meditation. I had noticed a piano in the corner of the room when I first walked in. "I'll play for a few minutes," I say.

I sit at the piano, and silently ask for help. For the next few minutes I play, and mercifully, the kitchen crew then finishes. We meditate for eight minutes in silence. After the meditation, I ask if anyone has anything they want to share. No one speaks. We sit quietly for a few minutes. And then Ellen says she wants to tell us what happened while she listened to the music.

I saw myself in a dark hole, but then I came out
of it and flew with the birds. I then realized that
I wanted to help women, and took them by the

hand and said, "You don't need to go down there,
but can fly too." They were able to fly, and then I
landed on the ground. I stood before a woman. It
made me realize that the dark hole, where I had
gone, gave me the thrust to reach the light. And
other women don't need to do it that way.

Behind Ellen's experience was a story of long-term abuse. She had fled, found the shelter, and regained her dignity. Her speaking from vulnerability created an opening, and the women in the circle began to talk and share of their own lives. The wisdom that arises in these situations is alive. It is the fruit or flowering that occurs when devotion is allowed to guide.

TO KNOW WHO I AM

ALIA CAME TO OUR MEETINGS for four months. Of Native American and French heritage, she has high cheek-bones and shoulder-length dark hair that frames the warmth of her smile. Alia works in community gardens. I was always happy to see her, and the other women respected her. Following silent meditation, Alia speaks.

After our last meeting when you talked about service, the next morning I woke up and the first thing I thought was, 'How can I serve? How can I serve God?' And then my roommate said that we needed to finish the 12 Steps. I realized that I could serve by taking care of my own healing. I need to do this so I can know who I am.

Alia was a woman of great strength, with a strong presence. To me it seemed that our circle helped her connect to an understanding that was linked to her own wholeness, that she had to say yes to what was in front of her, facing all the difficulties of addiction, and becoming sober, as a part of her devotion to her inner nature, to what is true in her life.

BELONGING

I felt so alone. There are so many people, and so little connection. But after I came here, I felt like I was connected. I felt my feet on the ground. I felt my heart beating. I felt connected to something. I was a part of it.

— TARA, homeless for two weeks, living in a large shelter

⇛⇚

People go to the edge of everything, when they sense the culture is not welcoming.

— ORLAND BISHOP, founder of Shade Tree
Multicultural Foundation

I HAVE THIS INSIDE

MY CO-FACILITATOR NANCY and I sit waiting for the women to arrive. Unlike the program at the daytime shelter which has the benefit of a central meeting place, here the women are told about our circles by case workers who suggest they come. When the women file into this small, windowless room, we are meeting them for the first time.

It's the only quiet room in this shelter that serves 150 men and women. I light a candle. It is the third meeting here. I feel a sensation of uneasiness in the pit of my stomach. The way it's set up here, we have no way to be with women prior to the meetings. They don't get to know us. So we sit here, waiting, not sure who will come. We rely on the caseworkers who steer the women in our direction, suggesting they come to our meetings. Will this work?

Just then, Evie walks in. She has come every time. She smiles broadly, and sees the empty chairs in the circle. She's thrilled, she says. She wants to talk to us, to tell us something but she didn't want to speak in front of the other women who came before.

Evie wears jeans and a green sweater, the color of spring. There is a brightness about her. An inquisitiveness, an openness to learn. Evie is thirty-nine.

I'm glad to be here. We touch life. That's what I learn from here, about the heart. I learn that it's

not only for me. I share. We share. This is how
people are touched. These tools I never learned
before, not even in counseling. These are special
tools I can practice. When I'm not in this circle, I
can practice.

She asks if she can just talk to us, and so we welcome her.
I lean back in my chair and listen.

Evie leans forward and begins to speak about her life.
How she was a girl in Mexico, who knew who she was at
an early age. "I used to sit by the ocean. I was calm. I had
peace. But then I lost it." Evie continues, wandering along
the path of her life, winding forwards to the present, back
to her early childhood, returning to her current situation.

She lost her job. Her husband no longer wanted to live
with her. Her teenage daughter now lives with cousins.
She works in the kitchen at the shelter because she wants
to give back. But she's getting tired. It has been just three
weeks since she was able to move to the shelter. Evie has
never been homeless before.

I keep my eyes on Evie as she talks on and on, filling
the room with a restless wandering through her life. She
skirts around several traumas, only hinting at them. There
is not a pause, a breath. I crave an open window, a waft of
fresh air.

I have a gut sense to allow her this space. Not to interrupt her. But it feels almost unbearable to hear her stories,
broken fragments of a life.

Evie stops talking for a few seconds. It's the first opening. I say to Evie, "Can you focus on your *Yes*? Something in you knows. Then you can value it." Nancy, who is a midwife, begins to speak quietly to Evie. She says that she sees such longing in her life. It's like a thread, she says, that has run through her life since she was a young girl, all the way until today. It's a thread of longing.

Evie's eyes focus on us. She is suddenly completely present. This is why she gets up in the early morning to sit in the bathroom where it's quiet, she says. She needs this time to sit still. I say, "That's your *santuario!*" Her sanctuary, her refuge. Now we are all laughing. A lightness has entered the room, and with it, an element of the invisible.

There is a pause, a silence in the room. Evie leans back in her seat. Her hands rest easily on her lap. Her eyes are now closed. We all sit quietly for a few minutes of meditation. And then Evie opens her eyes again, and she is nodding, as if confirming what she somehow already knew.

I knew I had something but it always came and went, and I didn't know what it was. But now you have given me words, given me a language, and now I know that I have this inside. It is mine. This place, this peace. Everyone should know this. Now I have a word. A language. Otherwise I wouldn't know it. I have this inside.

I talked about my difficulties with friends, but afterwards nothing happens and I feel agitated. But today after talking I feel peaceful, and this is new.

THIS FLOWER IS ME

WHEN I FIRST SEE MEI, she is sitting on a bench in
the courtyard of the shelter wearing a pale yellow twin
sweater set with gray slacks. Her skin is smooth and clear.
I guess she is in her late forties. I approach her and ask
if she would like to join the women's meditation group.
Without hesitation, she says, "Yes."

For a time, she comes every week to our meetings. In
the circles, we never ask the women about their lives. They
share when they feel safe. Mei speaks little over the first
few months, but one day she talks to me after our meeting and confides that she is Chinese but grew up in Vietnam. After the war, she moved to the United States to live
with her husband, but the relationship ended. She became
homeless one year ago.

One day I pass around cards with images of flowers
and ask the women to pick one that speaks to them. Mei
chooses a yellow wildflower and speaks quietly, but with
conviction.

*Some people have tried to make me feel bad about
myself. They try to put me down. I realized when
we were meditating, that this flower is me.*

Soon after that meeting, Mei needs to move to another
shelter. Their requirements prevent her from attending

our Thursday morning circle. A year passes, and then, one cold morning, when I glance outside a few minutes before the circle starts, someone who looks very much like Mei is crossing the courtyard.

I rush out to greet her. She's wearing a black business jacket and heels, light makeup and pale pink lipstick. "Mei!"

We embrace. Mei says, "I'm nervous. I have two interviews today, but I wanted to come to the group. Maybe it will help me."

Mei sits with seven other women in the circle. Even before we begin introductions, Mei speaks with an urgency I hadn't heard before from her. "Last night I had a dream. Can I tell it? I have to leave early because of the interviews."

I am on a sinking ship, so afraid, and I cry, "Help!" but no one helps me. I hear voices humming, like singing, all around me but I see no one. Why don't they come help? I would help someone if they were sinking. I cry out again, "Help!" but no one comes. I just hear the humming, singing all around me. I woke up so upset, crying. Does this mean I'm going to sink?

This is the first dream that she's shared with the circle and, for a moment, I don't know how to respond. One of the women says she needs a glass of water and leaves the room. I sense that Mei's dream is too close to the bone. Ginny, who has practiced Zen for forty years, begins to speak softly.

There is help all around us. This dream is a reminder that we're being held by the spirit, however you understand this. We are being held so beautifully.

Angels have always been portrayed as singing, or humming—an invisible vibration of divine love. We have so much fear, but in the dream the angels are singing.

Visibly calmed, Mei nods, saying, "I pray for myself. I pray for the world and for others not to be homeless." Her face shines, her nervousness has vanished. With a solidity, she says, "I knew I needed to come here this morning. Now I can go to my interviews."

Several months later, I'm walking in my neighborhood and see a woman getting out of her car in front of a house down the road from my own. I call out, "Mei?" She looks up and greets me in return. Right there on the street, we give a quick hug.

She tells me that she now works full-time for an agency that provides in-home eldercare. My reasoning mind struggles with the symbolism of the yellow wildflower that she had chosen in our circle so long ago. In a potentially stressful job, would she be able to live this quality that belongs to her natural self, closer to her than her breath? Then I remember: Mei prays for the world. She is held by her sense of belonging.

LOST AND FOUND

IN AN OFFICE overlooking redwood trees and Highway 101, I meet a new group of women who do not know each other. They are mostly mothers in their twenties and thirties, all indigenous women. Most are at risk of homelessness, even though they currently have housing. This is our first circle here. I light a candle.

Introducing myself, I mention my connection to the organization hosting the circle through an indigenous elder whose granddaughter worked there. This elder's friendship had helped me deeply during a difficult and lonely time in my life. I tell them I had wanted to come hold this circle as a way of giving back.

And then, as we go around the circle, each woman tells a story. The first sits beside a child's car seat cradling an infant girl, who has the dark brown eyes of her mother. Carmen fidgets and adjusts the blanket. She also has a four-year-old son, she says. Right now they are living with relatives, but it's noisy. She gestures as she talks, waving her hands to show the chaos. She wants to find a job and pay for her own place with her children.

The woman sitting beside Carmen nods in agreement and eagerly takes her turn. Nora tells us that she and her child live in an apartment. She doesn't have next month's rent. The others share just a little, but the stories are laced largely with the same difficulties—relatives, rent, running on empty. One woman feels numbness after a broken marriage.

None of the women have meditated before, but they all slip easily into the silence which pervades the room. After five minutes, I introduce the writing practice, and the women reach out with interest as I hand around pads of paper and pens. I give a writing prompt *Once there was a seed*. Or, you can begin with *Once there was a flower*. Write whatever words come to you, I say. Don't judge at all.

As they write, the baby drifts to deep sleep and Carmen appears calm. This calm spreads through the circle. Every woman is writing her own story.

Seven minutes later, I invite them to read their writing, if they want to. "I'll go," Carmen says, "I didn't know I could write like this."

Once there was a seed that was planted by a river by a person who wanted to see what it would grow into. The seed was watered by the rain and was kept moist by the mist of the river. The person did not return to where he planted the seed for many years. When he did return, the seed was not as he expected. He thought he would see a tree or beautiful flowers, or something similar. But all he saw was a shriveled up plant that appeared neglected and lonely. Maybe the person should have taken the time to learn what the seed was, and see what environment it would thrive in, before he planted it, to ensure its survival.

The women's faces show surprise. This story, that seems to have come out of nowhere, needs no interpretation and touches us all. Though we have agreed to listen without comment, Nora can't hold back. "That's so deep. How did you think of that?"

I heard in Carmen's story of abandonment the fundamental human longing, the calling within life, to restore our sense of belonging.

Another woman in her late twenties, a mother of two, is keen to read next. "It's weird," she says apologetically. "It doesn't mean anything." But her face is aglow.

Once there was a flower who was a grumpy flower. His leaves were turning brown. His petals started to fall off. So he just kept getting mad and didn't understand why these things were happening to him. So one day he picked up his roots and he moved to the other side of the park where the playground was. As he planted his roots down and saw all those kids playing, he began to relax and enjoy the sounds, the sunshine. Then a little girl was going around smelling the flowers and noticed that he was turning brown. So she pulled out her water bottle and sprinkled some water on him, and as she walked away this grumpy old flower was smiling and she came back every day and gave him some water until he turned into a beautiful flower.

The story speaks of how this woman too, had started to find her belonging—the little girl inside her had noticed the withered flower, and was watering it!

I think of the women as a clan of teachers. Within their stories of loss and of being found, I notice the seeds of new consciousness.

Reflection

MY DREAM:
I am shown a vast, living, interconnected fabric made up of intersecting lines. It is pulsating with life force—dynamic and alive. It looks like white lace, only it is made out of light. Each woman, I am told, has her own unique pattern that is formed out of her life. The separate pieces of each woman's life need to be stitched together, so that their individual patterns become part of the whole. I am told that this is how women work together.

This dream helped me understand more deeply the importance of how women need to find their belonging. We all need to sense the whole of which we are a part, so as not to feel overly burdened by the separateness and aloneness of our times and our culture. Sitting in circles, focusing on the sacred within, alone and together, repeatedly we see how we are part of and belong to life.

THE MISSING PIECE

ON A WARM SUMMER evening, sixty volunteers and staff gather together for the day shelter's annual volunteer party in a noisy assembly hall. I don't recognize anyone except for the program director, who had invited me to give a brief talk on our program. Men and women mill around long tables, eating vegetables and dip, hummus and chips, drinking wine or juices.

The director makes a few announcements and then invites the speakers—myself and another—to the front of the room. I was to go second. The first, a well-dressed woman, tells us about her daughter, who had died the previous week. She had fallen and been found in a tent in a street park. The daughter was a cellist who had studied at the San Francisco Music Conservatory. The mother thanks every person who touched her daughter in some way. The emotion in the room is palpable; we are all moved by the mother's vulnerability.

When I step up next to talk about our program at the shelter, I feel like I'm speaking into a huge heart. I begin by explaining how the pilot project that was going to last for six week has now lasted five years. I hold up a brochure we used initially, but then hadn't needed. Once women heard about the circle through word of mouth, they were drawn to it.

As I speak, I look around the room at all the faces, several that I now recognize—volunteers, staff. I empty myself of ideas I had prepared to share in my talk and, instead, share with the audience what we do each Thursday morning in our circles. I talk about discovering how much the women yearn for silence, and a sanctuary where they could think and reflect on their lives, and their next steps. How as facilitators, we hold the understanding that every woman is a sacred being. Each woman has wisdom inside. Over time, we have witnessed them access that wisdom.

A woman sitting at a table suddenly waves her hand in the air. "I need to say something."

Two years ago I was standing outside the church in the early evening. I saw a woman sitting on the steps. I thought to myself that she was homeless, and I judged her. I felt fear. But then the woman spoke. And I forgot all about it, but I remembered it when you were talking.

She said to me, "We need to listen to each other. God put wisdom into the hearts of each one of us. We must listen to each other."

I'm sorry to interrupt, but I had to say this. She' s saying exactly what you're saying!

The feeling in the room changes. A space opens. Quiet, stillness. I then tell stories about the women who have participated in our program. I speak about our experiences, and read the writing of the women. They have given me permission to share what they wrote, I say. The quietness remains, settling in the room. I explain that the women we meet tell us that they do not want to be known as 'homeless women.' Instead, they think of themselves as women in transition. It has been an honor to sit with these women, I say. They face enormous obstacles and challenges, but are willing to sit together, to listen to each other and inside themselves. They access their own wisdom, and are amazed to find value in themselves, in their wisdom and sacredness.

After I finish, a young man approaches me. "I had no idea this was going on here." Then a retired businessman speaks to me and says that he didn't know this depth was taking place at the shelter. He wants to tell me how he volunteers every Monday as a cook for the meals served at the shelter. But hearing about the women makes him feel that he's part of a larger work. He shakes his head in amazement. It is, to him, like finding the missing piece of a mosaic.

WE MUST WORK TOGETHER

CONSTANCE WEARS A WOVEN cotton shawl over an embroidered shirt and khaki colored slacks, and comes in late. She enters with a certain self-respect or sense of maturity, finds an empty chair, and sits quietly. Her hair is pulled back in a loose ponytail. She appears to be in her late forties or early fifties. For some reason, I notice her shoes—sturdy and practical, with laces. After she settles, she focuses on listening.

I brought a quote to read this day, words from Larry Merculieff, an Aleut elder, trained primarily by the grandmothers of his tribe. He speaks on behalf of the great need of our time to reconnect with the earth and the sacred feminine. I read aloud his words as a way to introduce a deeper understanding of the need for each woman to find her empowerment,

> *Women now are being called to restore their own center of power. Because even with all of this violence that has been done to women for thousands of years, they still hold the sacredness within them.*

Then we meditate. In the silence, a quiet peace seems to expand and fill the space. Afterwards, I open the circle for a time to talk freely, using the talking piece that we pass around.

Several women have been moved by the quote from Larry Merculieff, and a lively discussion follows about the economy, the environment, and how they feel the impact of global change. Constance, who sits on the other side of the circle, in her shawl and thoughtful expression, breaks her silence. Her soft voice rises and falls in a gentle melody, yet there is a rock-like strength as she speaks.

It is said in our prophecy that people must work together. We need to make our physical bodies strong and work together with God. But people don't understand. Many people say, "Why should I do that? It doesn't make any difference." I tell you, the world will need this.

The women in the circle listen with attention. As if life is speaking to life. At this moment, there is very little sense of the personal. We have been given a global perspective. This does not come from me, or another facilitator. We simply hold the space.

We then have a minute of silence, which is how we always end the hour-long circle. The silence reverberates. Life energy has entered this small gathering, and touches each of us.

It's nearly time for lunch. The women gather their backpacks and purses, and I notice their companionship, which is new, which has come out of their shared experience today. It's as if silent prayers have been offered in the sharing, as if hearts have been woven together.

HEALING THE SOUL
OF THE WORLD

*I had a vision that the ancestors told us to heal the world.
When we heal ourselves, we also heal our ancestors, our
grandmothers, our grandfathers, and our children. When
we heal ourselves, we also heal Mother Earth.*

—Grandmother Rita Pitka Blumenstein

*What came out of my experience being homeless is that
I want to be of service.*

—Trina, speaking to the women in the circle

AT A RECENT GROUNDBREAKING ceremony for a new homeless shelter, I spoke briefly to the community. I said that one of the meanings of groundbreaking is to prepare for seeds that will later nourish people. We care for the seeds by watering, protecting, and tending the plant as it grows. The new shelter, in the same way, will be the ground for planting seeds with the women and the children it serves, as they re-grow their lives out of the challenges they face now.

That night, after the ceremony, I had a dream. In it I see a silver vial holding a special substance. The vial is feminine in shape, like the perfume vials of earlier times. I see these words: "For the future." To me this served to affirm how the work with women is seeding the future—a future founded in feminine wisdom, grounded in the sacred source from which we all come.

The women whose stories we have heard are each beginning to find their way to an inner home that they can tap into when needed. As is true for all of us, without connecting with this inner essence, we cannot move forward in a world that cries out for us to remember our wholeness.

After meditation one day during the time that I was writing this book, I suggested that the women begin their writing practice with *Once there was a garden*. Carrie, who had been homeless for half a year, and who said that she comes to the circle for the quiet, read aloud first.

Once there was a garden with rows and rows of plants, flowers, and on the edges, trees. Once there was a garden, plants with food, people came to pick, where people met, told stories and fell in love. The trees stood tall with their roots firmly planted, and the plants standing firm, bearing food. Flowers bloomed as wildlife lived near. The squirrels living in the tall trees, bees getting pollen from the flowers on bright sunny days. Once there was a garden filled with life, love and compassion that can still be here to this day.

Carrie described an inner garden, breathing with possibility and life energy. Her story offered more than a personal meaning, because it was about oneness—an unspoken, living connection linked with every part of creation.

In our circles we help each other move beyond the place of isolation and fragmentation that weakens us as individuals and as community. We silently acknowledge the healing and regenerative capacity within us, and the flow of life that runs through us.

As these stories spill like seeds out from this book to the wider collective, I hope they help women connect to the heart of life everywhere, especially in the ordinary tasks we each have to meet each day. My wish is that we all find the courage to heal the soul of the world, by taking our place within this new possibility of oneness being born in our time.

PRACTICAL POINTS

CREATING CIRCLES

The following is excerpted from an email exchange I had with a South African woman, now working with marginalized women in Australia.

GETTING STARTED

Q: *Because I know from your website that you host circles for homeless women's shelters, I am hoping you could share, in your experience, how you created the space to offer a circle for women which focuses on the inner, in a sector which predominantly focuses on the external, such as advocacy and policy issues.*

Could you share how you partnered with community organizations to enable women to access their deep knowing through the circles? I am assuming that it was through personal relationships, where women who were in these organizations, expressed a need.

A: Yes, this did come about through relationships. I approached a women's day shelter after meeting a former board member who said she would introduce me to the program director. It took several meetings over several months with this program director—she was very busy, but also this work was not in her frame of reference. Once she opened to it, however, I saw she was highly intuitive and deeply devoted to the women. She became an ally in the sense that she encourages women to come to the circles when she thinks they would benefit.

After we began the circle, it was clearly evident that the women benefitted in a deep and powerful way. The women themselves suggested that we contact other shelters. So we went to three other shelters and offered the program at these new locations. Without a personal reference, I eventually approached the largest shelter in the county, and spoke to a case manager who seemed to understand the value of the circles. There I met with the shelter's executive director, who at first was highly resistant. I persisted in the conversation, and he too finally understood.

When I first start at a shelter, I offer a pilot project for six weeks, to see if it will help the women. It is safe that way, contained. But my primary project has now continued for over five years. I see that we could be doing this in every shelter in the county, because there is such need and the women are so hungry for the silence and open acceptance they receive in the circle.

The first time I ever spoke at a shelter, it was to introduce the program. I stood in front of forty-five women and was quite nervous. These women are on the streets, in shelters, or living in cars. But I somehow knew that I had to be absolutely transparent with them. So I began to talk about my experiences with women in other countries around the world, and how there has been so much suffering among women. How through these difficult times, women are finding their own sense of value and empowerment. I spoke about how every woman is sacred, and that this is something we have forgotten in the West. I also shared a few dreams that led me to working with women.

Something happened in that talk. I cannot explain it other than the room became absolutely still—not the slightest movement. The women were all looking at me with eyes that went beyond them. It was as if in that moment of stillness, *life* was listening. The staff later told me that they had never heard such stillness in that room. I realized that no one had ever reflected to the women that they are sacred. But it also seemed to go beyond the women in this room.

One of the Native American women came up to me after my talk and asked if she could tell me a dream. She had told this dream to psychologists and therapists but no one had ever been able to help her understand it. She then told the dream. I knew it came from her Native American ancestors trying to help her. I suggested this to her, and she knew, instantly, that it was correct. I took this as an indication to begin the circles and to trust. It is not easy. Sometimes women, like her, are dealing with serious addictions. But often the women who come to our circles are on a healing path, and are able to move out of homelessness.

There is more receptivity to this work now because what I see is that organizations are more receptive to help from the community. They cannot deal on their own with the increasing need as social structures collapse and change. There is an opening now that I did not feel ten years ago.

I also gave a presentation to the staff at the shelter, after a year. Before I left my house that day, I lay down for just a few minutes, hoping to figure out how I would speak to them. I must have fallen asleep, for when I was waking, I heard, "*Let it be...*" I realized it was from the Beatles song about Mother Mary. I felt a great solace and strength. I could trust the moment rather than figure out what I was going to say. It was only a twenty-minute presentation, and I decided to invite the women into the experience of our circles. It touched them deeply. After that, they were very supportive of my work there.

Another form of outreach I used was to develop a simple brochure, which helped initially. In the brochure I describe the mission of the program in this way: *to provide tools and cultivate inner resources that empower women to meet and transform the challenges they face. For many, the program is key to making the transition to live in a different, more sustainable way.* I also began to mentor several women in these circles. I found that there is such a need for the circles, and you will probably find that too when you host your own circles.

CONTENT AND FORMAT

Q: *It is so incredible to hear how all the steps unfolded in this wondrous way, and also to hear about the steps you took practically, one at a time, from building the relationships with allies, to the pilots, and now including mentoring others to host circles, four years later. And all the while the silence and acceptance at the heart and center of it all.*

Could you please share about the content and duration of the sessions: about how much time might one spend in silence, on the women's sharing about themselves, and how much on dream work?

A: I began thinking that these would be circles for dream work. In fact, that did interest women because they had quite strong dreams with no understanding of their significance or meaning. But very soon after, it changed. Life seemed to have had another idea, which had more to do with women experiencing being welcomed at the level of the soul, simply through being together, sharing, and creativity. It unfolded without any agenda.

I realized that the images that came in meditation also needed to be included. And now, often, the women will share an image that arose during the meditation that has great significance to their lives. Dreams are still included if they come up, however.

As to the format: We have just one hour together. The chairs are in a circle, and a candle is lit. If I have time, I bring a few flowers in a vase. One of the most potent aspects of this work is beauty. There is so little beauty in the women's lives.

I begin with an introduction. I share a little about myself, and I give a copy of my book, *Women, Wisdom, and Dreams*, to those who don't have it. (I have been given a grant to share the books in this way.) This introduction helps the women to feel some trust, and to know that someone is not going to try to impose on them. An example of the feeling of this talk is what a young woman from Micronesia told me a few weeks ago, after the circle. "Thank you for welcoming me." It is this welcoming and acceptance at a very deep level that is so rare and precious to the women.

Then the women go around the circle, tell their name, and have an opportunity to share a little about why they are here at the circle or something about themselves. This needs to be focused. I have them use a talking piece, which they hold while sharing, and explain that there is no cross talk during this time. We just listen. It is good for the women to hold something in their hand as they speak. We have used a polished pink heart stone and, for a while, we used a figurine we found in the room. It must have been a depiction of Mary, but it looked like Kwan Yin.

Sometimes what is shared is very moving, and I get a sense of the need of this particular group of women during that time.

Then, we usually have our meditation. Often I use a simple heart meditation. Beforehand, I also include aware-ness of the breath, like the ocean waves. If there is a lot of agitation, then I will sometimes ask my colleague to lead the meditation she offers, which is a grounding meditation, connecting to the earth.

When we're finished, the feeling is always deeper, more still, and the women are more quiet within them-selves. Then we have time to share about the experience of meditation, or images that came up, or a dream. At times a woman will come to the circle filled with eagerness because she had a dream and wants to share it. Then we speak about it, and help her to connect to it, and find meaning. Or, it might be an image in meditation. I find that it's hard for the women to remember their dreams if they aren't sleeping well in a noisy shelter. There is less focus on dreams for this reason.

After a year of these circles, I began to incorporate the tool of writing in the circles. I invite the women to write, suggesting they begin with a phrase, such as *Once there was a girl...* or *Once there was a tree...* I sometimes bring some beautiful cards with photographs of flowers. The beauty evokes the women's own beauty, working like a contemplation to spring from. I then invite them to write for five to ten minutes.

There is a story in the women that often emerges during this time. They carry such a deep knowing, and once they start to value it, they seem eager to communicate it.

The atmosphere in the room becomes very clear and peaceful. After this time, I ask if they would like to read aloud. They are completely free to share or not to share. But nearly everyone wants to read what they have written. It is empowering in a profound way. I emphasize that we are just to listen, not to comment. I am repeatedly astonished to witness the beauty and wisdom inside the women. Sometimes, the energy is so full that the women can barely contain themselves, and then they talk freely. And then a certain aliveness—even joy and laughter—

sometimes arises spontaneously. The role of the facilitator here is a matter of both holding and allowing.

Then I close the circle with a minute of silence, and there is a different quality now after the hour. There is often a deep peace, and the women don't seem to want to leave it quickly.

For the first year, I held the circles on my own. But working with women in transition, who are experiencing so many types of energetic difficulties, I realized it is helpful—if possible—to have someone to assist in these circles. I invited other women co-facilitators I know (both friends and colleagues) to hold the space with me.

To summarize, the format loosely follows this sequence:

INTRODUCTIONS—We each give our name and a brief introduction around the circle. I ask, "What brought you here? Or what intention do you have for today?" In the first year, women needed to have a focus or else the introduction would last for too long. Now, the women are more concise about what would help them in the circle.

TOPIC—I speak about a seed topic, or read a poem or other writing.

MEDITATION— We sit for 5–10 minutes in silence.

SHARING—We tell the stories that arose in the meditation. It's important to listen without commenting.

WRITING—We write for up to 10 minutes on the topic. (optional)

CLOSING—Usually with a brief silence of a minute or so.

There are variations, but this is the essential structure.

Q: *It's so encouraging to know what is possible, and what has worked well for the women. Your work is making the invisible more visible and creating the opportunities for others to find the courage to create these spaces where we previously thought it would be met with resistance, and yet where they are so needed and so received.*

A: Thank you.

WHY MEDITATION?

I've never sat for five minutes in my life with my eyes closed. I saw my children happy, my brother, who taught me about life. I felt him behind me. And then I saw a light on my right. I thought this is the brain making this up. But it wasn't. Then I saw darkness for a moment but I said, no, I'm going to the light. I'm turning my attention to the light, it might have been bad thoughts. It left.

—JOANNA, mother of two grown children, newly homeless

I was afraid to meditate. I felt that if I gave up control over my mind then things would fall apart. I felt that I needed to keep on top of things because I'm so close to getting my children back. But this is different. I've never felt anything like this.

—TAMARA, homeless for one year

In the meditation, I put people in my heart that I love. And then I saw a dove. I tried to make it go away but it wouldn't. What is this? Does this mean something's wrong? Aren't doves supposed to be in pairs?

—CAROL, newly homeless

THE STILL CENTER

WHAT DOES MEDITATION do for women, for those who might even just be sleeping or resting, and for those who make immediate contact with their inner life through imagery or other felt experiences? There's an interesting range of ways it touches women, and a place for all to be met there.

In the circles at the shelters, even in these brief meditations which last five to ten minutes, the women drop into a deep state within themselves—even those who have never experienced meditation. Many of the women are dealing with anxiety, restlessness, and sometimes, pain. So I usually suggest five minutes of meditation, but if the silence is very deep, we go longer. It is quite amazing that this brief amount of time is enough to touch their depths. Meditation can be very effective in helping women reach that still, silent center of their being.

If the women have been traumatized, then sitting still for much longer than this may be difficult. I remember one woman who said she had never sat still in her whole life. She was very resistant and had a lot of anger. But she, like other women, came out of meditation and said softly, what *was* that? Often, the women have never touched this place of peace in them, and this changes the way they think of themselves.

There are many forms of meditation. Always, we encourage women to use whatever practice they are most comfortable with, but we also share a simple heart meditation if they wish. For in the circle, nothing is imposed. We create a safe container in which the women can feel and hear their inner knowing.

Sometimes, an image arises in a woman's meditation. Usually such images nourish us. Even if we don't understand its symbolic meaning, it still speaks, or carries an energy, that we can receive deep into our being. These images actually bridge the inner dimension with our outer life. They hold a regenerative energy that can heal at the level of the soul. It might be for just a moment, or it can last for days, helping us to make a better decision, or shift our attitude about ourself or life.

There is always a certain wonder in the grace of meditation. I remember a woman in her early thirties, who was new to the circle. Pulled down by several months of homelessness, she was willing to try meditation. It might help her mind, she said, with its ceaseless worry and agitation. After we meditated, she shared,

I imagined myself walking towards a stream, because that's where I often feel love, by the water. But then I was no longer imagining anything. I was in the stream alongside hundreds of salmon all swimming towards the ocean. I was a salmon! At first I was afraid because there was so much energy. It was so dynamic and all the fish were moving fast, together. But then I stopped being afraid. I felt so free, and joyful. I can still feel it. I've never had anything like this before.

Her face was so bright! A visible change had occurred, and it touched all the women in the circle. And now I share it with you who read this book. Sometimes I feel like these stories are like little lights that glimmer in the dark. They show us what's possible. And they help us to remember this wonder, this depth, inside each of us.

MEDITATION OF THE HEART

Become aware of your breath, in and out, like gentle waves at the ocean. Now, think of someone you love. Or a time you felt moved by nature, like watching a sunset or standing at the ocean. However you feel this love, which is unique for each of us, place this feeling in your heart. As thoughts arise in the mind, just drop them into the heart, one by one, like dropping pebbles into a pond.

And then we rest in the silence.

ACKNOWLEDGMENTS

My DEEPEST GRATITUDE to Diana Badger, editor and friend, who skillfully and with great sensitivity edited and wove the stories and reflections in this book together. Her insights, along with her compassionate facilitation of circles with homeless women, have proven invaluable to the creation of this book.

Gratitude also to Ginny Myosho Matthews, colleague and friend, who joined me in co-facilitating the circles in the shelter. It has been a joy to work together, and I am grateful for her steadfast love for the women, and for the work itself. Thank you also to Nancy O'Brien, for co-facilitating our program at a new shelter. Her depth of experience and understanding of women in transition was a gift. Also, my respect and gratitude to Maggie Caffery, who has worked as a group facilitator with faithful commitment and love.

A deep acknowledgement of Celeste Austin, Director of Special Programs, whose intuition always steered the right women in our direction. To Lynda Terry, who has supported this work since the beginning, thank you. And to Jennifer Badde-Graves, for her steadfast support.

With my gratitude to both Ilarian Larry Merculieff at the Global Center for Indigenous Leadership and Lifeways, and to Orland Bishop, founder of ShadeTree Multicultural Foundation.

Finally, to the women who participated in our circles, thank you from my heart.

ABOUT THE AUTHOR

ANNE SCOTT, founder of DreamWeather Foundation, has led workshops and retreats for women in diverse communities and organizations around the country and internationally. The focus of her work is restoring the link between feminine wisdom and social change, and the healing nature of dreams. Anne was a speaker at the United Nations Peace Initiative in Geneva, Switzerland, in 2002, and a global conference in Jaipur, India: *Making Way for the Feminine for the Benefit of the World Community*, in 2008. She also co-led a workshop at the 2015 Parliament of World Religions in Salt Lake City: *Embodied Service— The Wholeness of Women's Spiritual Leadership.*

Anne is the author of several books, including *Women, Wisdom & Dreams: The Light of the Feminine Soul,* and *Serving Fire: Food for Thought, Body and Soul.* She began working with groups of newly homeless women in shelters in 2010. The core of her work is restoring the sacred to life through embodying ancient feminine wisdom.

You can reach Anne at:
DreamWeather Foundation
P.O. Box 2002
Sebastopol, CA 95473

www.dreamweather.org
info@dreamweather.org

CPSIA information can be obtained
at www.ICGtesting.com
Printed in the USA
FSOW01n1549280616
22123FS